THE ANOINTING OF
HIS SPIRIT

The Anointing of His Spirit

Smith Wigglesworth

Compiled and Edited by
Wayne Warner

VINE
BOOKS

Servant Publications
Ann Arbor, Michigan

All Scripture quotations are taken from *The King James Bible.*

Vine Books is an imprint of Servant Publications
especially designed to serve evangelical Christians.

Published by Servant Publications
P.O. Box 8617
Ann Arbor, Michigan 48107

Cover design by Eric Walljasper

     96 97 98 10 9 8 7 6 5

Printed in the United States of America
ISBN 0-89283-863-9

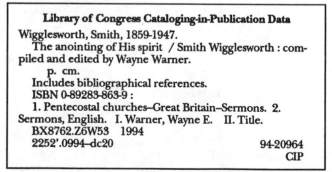

Library of Congress Cataloging-in-Publication Data
Wigglesworth, Smith, 1859-1947.
    The anointing of His spirit / Smith Wigglesworth : com-
piled and edited by Wayne Warner.
        p. cm.
    Includes bibliographical references.
    ISBN 0-89283-863-9 :
    1. Pentecostal churches–Great Britain–Sermons. 2.
Sermons, English. I. Warner, Wayne E.   II. Title.
    BX8762.Z6W53   1994
    2252'.0994–dc20   94-20964
                                                              CIP

To Pat

for her prayer and encouragement
beginning when this book project
was no more than a dream.

APPRECIATION

To two people who immersed themselves in Wigglesworth sermons to give this book a quality that it otherwise would not have:

Glenn Gohr spent many hours searching through magazines—some of which were published as early as 1907—for Wigglesworth sermons, and then compared my initial selection to make certain that I had not chosen sermons that were already in book form. He also deleted illustrations which Wigglesworth used more than once in the final selection.

Mary Kay Glunt accepted the challenge of electronically scanning the old sermon pages, "cleaning" them, and then placing them on floppy disks so that I could prepare them for this book—an electronic procedure unheard of in Wigglesworth's time.

Appreciation is also due Servant Publications editor Beth Feia for suggesting this compilation, not aware that I had already been thinking of such a book. Her spark ignited the fire.

CONTENTS

FOREWORD

A Pentecostal Phenomenon[1]
by Donald Gee

SMITH WIGGLESWORTH HAS BECOME A LEGEND.

I am relieved that my present congenial task consists only of recording some personal memories. It was his great admirer Stanley H. Frodsham who wrote the well-known pentecostal best-seller *Ever-Increasing Faith* from stories supplied by Wigglesworth.[2]

Lacking the advantage of an early education, this plumber-preacher read little but the Bible throughout his lifetime. Yet Wigglesworth possessed natural qualities that made him one of God's gentlemen. He was always well dressed and took great care of himself. He gave this word of wisdom about making trips in reasonable comfort: "I'm saving the Lord's servant." His care yielded a dividend, for this tireless traveler lived to be nearly eighty-eight.

My earliest recollections were necessarily from a distance. Wigglesworth's platform style was unique. When preaching he would often become tangled in long, involved sentences. Then he would relieve the audience's perplexity by speaking angelically in tongues which he always interpreted himself. It was all part of the sermon. Explain it how you will, there were some remarkable flashes of revelation. The preacher himself probably little understood the sheer theological depth and insight of his own words.

Wigglesworth was truly a pentecostal phenomenon.

His favorite and almost his only subject was faith. No matter what the text, we all knew where he would arrive. He soon became dubbed "The Apostle of Faith."

Crowds flocked to his meetings for healing as the legend grew, especially in other lands. Earlier in his preaching career, Wigglesworth employed methods which were often rough. He was a powerfully built man who did not know his own strength. Diseases like cancer made this man of God blaze with holy anger. Very often he made people run up and down the aisles, and even out into the street, to "act" faith. His fierce laying on of hands would almost send the seeker flying, but he was intensely sincere.

My first intimate contact came when Wigglesworth stayed in our home in Edinburgh, during some special meetings in the assembly. While the manse on Scotland Street had to accommodate visitors who pleaded for a bed, this renowned preacher possessed a fascination for the cultured. My wife and I found him to be delightful: unselfish, courteous, generous, a man who filled the house with an aroma of the presence of God. We saw no miracles, but our souls were richly blessed by this godly servant.

Later on Wigglesworth suffered intense physical agony because of gallstones. As an act of faith, he refused to seek medical aid and continued his preaching, even though his clothing would become soaked with blood. His courage inspired all who saw him. The stones eventually passed, to the glory of God. I can never forget the night in Sion College, London, when Wigglesworth held up before the congregation a bottle that contained the horrid, jagged things. The preacher's ordeal had utterly broken his spirit, and we all shared his emotion. After that a new gentleness marked his praying for the sick.

A choice personal memory is connected with an Easter convention in Preston, England. I asked to be excused after the Good Friday service in order to speak at another convention. Wigglesworth objected very tartly, but a little later he humbly asked my forgiveness and apologized in a way that melted my heart.

The highlight of my personal fellowship with Smith Wigglesworth was the three Easters he spent in Preston. His chairmanship of a convention was a surprise to those who imagined that the famous preacher would insist on dominating the platform. To the contrary, he made ample room for his colleagues to minister and made things move like silk. He would be ruthless with any abuse of spiritual gifts and had no compunction about telling people to sit down and be quiet if not in the Spirit. And they took it—from Smith Wigglesworth!

Having spent the winter alone with God at his home in Bradford, the "Apostle of Faith" arrived at Easter anointed with fresh oil. Those were the last pentecostal conventions of the early type, the kind that another generation would never know. An era in the pentecostal movement passed with the death of Wigglesworth.

Little did I imagine that I would be with him when he died. Yet so it was. When his old friend Wilfred Richardson died in the terrible winter snow of 1947, Wigglesworth insisted on going to the March funeral at Wakefield. Climbing the steep flight of steps to the chapel in the bitter cold may have been too much for his heart. We were gathered in the vestry where a cheerful fire was burning. While waiting for the cortege, I asked my friend if he was warm. Wigglesworth replied, "I am warm." Those were his last words.[3] He gave a few gasps, and was gone. There was no struggle and no pain; it was a lovely passing. Quietly we laid him on the floor and kissed that noble brow. His

son-in-law, James Salter, fetched Alice Wigglesworth Salter from
out of the stunned congregation.

A few days later we buried the old warrior on a bright winter
afternoon in Bradford. I invited Joseph Smith, then dean of
Elim Bible College, to say a few words. He said, "We often hear
the remark, 'He's gone,' but in this case he has arrived. Brother
Wigglesworth was not an ordinary man, but extraordinary, and
it was his faith in God that made him so."

Those apt words summed up the character of this world-
famous evangelist. Whatever his faults, Smith Wigglesworth was
a man of God.

INTRODUCTION

If someone had prophesied to Smith Wigglesworth in 1914 that a publisher would reprint some of his sermons in eighty years, he no doubt would have considered that person a false prophet. First, he believed that born-again Christians would be caught up with the Lord long before the last decade of the century. Second, even if Christ had not yet returned, it would be inconceivable to him that his simple sermons would find a market nearly fifty years after his death.

He would have been wrong on both counts.

Believers—many of whom are baby boomers born after this preacher's death in 1947—still await Christ's return. A great number of these believers accept Smith Wigglesworth as the "Apostle of Faith." They view him as a unique pentecostal prophet and evangelist, and a predecessor of other evangelists who prayed for the sick. And they will read everything available about and by this former plumber of Bradford, England.

In contrast to the high-tech, televised healing services of recent years, Wigglesworth's quaint and picturesque language appears rather archaic. Yet his anointed sermons—coupled with the legends surrounding his ministry—give him appeal to every generation. Unfortunately, we have no known recordings or films of his colorful preaching and his unpredictable actions.

When eighteen of his sermons were taken down in shorthand and published as *Ever-Increasing Faith* in 1924, Wigglesworth wouldn't read them, preferring rather to read the Bible.

At least one other book of sermons, *Faith That Prevails,* was published during his lifetime. A third collection, *Cry of the Spirit,* was published in 1990. Some years before Wigglesworth died, he told a friend that royalties from *Ever-Increasing Faith* and *Faith That Prevails* were designated for foreign missions and that the books had already earned a total of fifty thousand dollars.[1]

As an editor for Gospel Publishing House in 1971, I wrote the foreword to a new edition of *Ever-Increasing Faith.* I had no idea that more than twenty years later I would collect more Wigglesworth sermons for the book you now hold. This compilation was selected from well-known as well as obscure periodicals, some of which ceased publication more than half a century ago.

As you probably realize, the spoken word often goes through changes when placed in print. This book is no exception. Stenographers scribbled Wigglesworth's sermons in shorthand, and then the material was often condensed and always edited for clarity. With the passing of years, some terms fall into disuse, so I have deleted or updated certain phrases. I have also deleted illustrations and points which were duplicated in other sermons of this collection. And to help you quickly grasp the contents of the sermons, titles have been updated and subheadings have been added. The messages remain the same; only the vehicle carrying the messages has been changed.

If Wigglesworth appears to contradict himself at various points in this collection, or if you question his interpretations and judgments, keep in mind that these sermons were preached over a period of more than thirty years. What a stenographer captured in 1914 might not necessarily have reflected the evangelist's views in 1947. When known, the date Wigglesworth preached each sermon is indicated in "The Man and His Message" at the end of each chapter.

I was humbled time and again as I selected words spoken in faraway places during the early part of this century—words which could bless and encourage people at the end of the century, and into the twenty-first. Few people would have the opportunity to search through libraries and archives for Wigglesworth sermons, but in this printed form his message can reach untold people of this and future generations.

With the publication of *Ever-Increasing Faith*, a writer for the *Pentecostal Evangel* predicted, "This is a book that will make people hungry for God, and one that we believe the Lord will greatly use." With apologies to that writer seven decades ago, I hope and pray that the same can be said of *The Anointing of His Spirit*. I have no illusions that the Bradford plumber—were he still alive—would read this collection any more than he would *Ever-Increasing Faith*. But I am hopeful that these sermons will bless people in the same countries in which they were first preached to our grandparents and great-grandparents, as well as readers in other countries who never heard of Smith Wigglesworth.

Several legends associated with Wigglesworth's ministry created a man who was far more perfect and overcoming than he would ever have claimed to be. He despised exaggerations, but that didn't stop writers and preachers from embellishing some of his already unbelievable stories of healings and conversions. Wigglesworth was human, as his contemporary Donald Gee says in the foreword, yet a man of faith who believed that God had chosen him for a special ministry. The preacher himself assured his listeners that he would be immortal only in his resurrected life.

Mortal, but certainly unusual. For starters, Wigglesworth was a plumber with no formal or theological education. Few could equal his evangelistic courage, even convincing people to pray the sinner's prayer while on their knees in railroad cars, on the street, and in other public places. And how about his legendary voice? Seeing his father-in-law leaving the dock for Australia the first time, Wigglesworth's son-in-law remarked, "He lifted his voice repeatedly in a series of hallelujahs, with a clarity and volume I have never seen equaled." The ship's captain also commented on his lungs of steel. On another occasion the preacher rocked a music hall with his shouts of hallelujah after listening to a presentation of Handel's *The Messiah*.

Theologically, some would definitely call Smith Wigglesworth unusual in his conviction that all believers could be baptized in the Holy Spirit and that God performed miracles now just as he did in the first century. Even some of his pentecostal friends questioned what they saw as extremes in his beliefs about healing, and cringed whenever he expressed anti-medical views. Despite those who disagreed with him, and the fact that he murdered his king's English, Wigglesworth could attract a crowd whether he was at home in Bradford or preaching in the open air of Sri Lanka or South Africa.

Something else which made this preacher unusual was his age when he launched an unplanned international ministry. At forty-eight, when most people are at least thinking about retirement, Wigglesworth's evangelistic career blossomed after he was baptized in the Spirit in Sunderland. He was fifty-five before he traveled to North America, and sixty-five when his first book of sermons was published—in a foreign country at that. And he still preached and prayed for the sick into his eighty-seventh year.

Two practices always marked Smith Wigglesworth's healing services around the world: the use of "faith" passages from the Word of God, and robust singing of gospel songs and hymns. These practices were prayerfully designed to inspire his hearers to turn from unbelief, or a passive faith, and to believe God for things they previously considered impossible. Without the reading or quoting of the Word and the singing, a service simply was not a Wigglesworth service. And the people who attended soon learned that one of his favorite Bible passages was the eleventh chapter of the Book of Hebrews. In fact, six of the messages in this collection are based on that particular chapter, none of which is the same.

Wigglesworth could easily identify with the men and women of Hebrews 11—from Abel to the prophets—who "through faith subdued kingdoms, wrought righteousness, obtained promises, stopped the mouths of lions, quenched the violence of fire, escaped the edge of the sword, out of weakness were made strong, waxed valiant in fight, turned to flight the armies of the aliens" (vs 33-34).

The "Apostle of Faith" himself had experienced some of the same victories, rejections, and sorrows that his role models from Hebrews had suffered. He often recounted stories of his victories to encourage the sick and suffering; he even lived on Victor Street in Bradford. But Wigglesworth seldom addressed the problem many still faced after attending one of his meetings: illnesses that did not leave when he prayed. He taught faith, deliverance, and healing—not learning to live with sickness. Yet his own daughter, Alice Salter, who assisted in the meetings, never was healed of her deafness. Wigglesworth lost his wife Polly in 1913, and two years later his son died.

Loneliness added to the sorrow when he chose to remain single the rest of his thirty-four years. "After [Polly's] funeral," he told a friend eleven years later, "I went back and lay on her grave. I wanted to die there." Wigglesworth said that God told him to leave the grave. "I told him that if he would give me a double portion of the Spirit—my wife's and my own—I would go and preach the gospel." God answered the plumber's prayer, but Wigglesworth added that he sailed the seas alone and often wept because of his loneliness.[2]

Loneliness was not the only hindrance the preacher-evangelist faced in his worldwide ministry. People who did not accept or understand his ministry ridiculed him in public and in the press. Others had him thrown in jail, and still others threatened his life. Whatever the opposition, Wigglesworth took consolation in his heroes of faith named in Hebrews 11. By God's grace he endeavored to match their faith, dedication, and courage. And with the anointing of the Spirit on his life, he determined that everyone who heard him would be nudged a little closer to the Savior and gain a stronger faith for the miraculous.

One of Wigglesworth's oft-quoted statements clarified his beliefs and calling: "Fear looks; faith jumps. Faith never fails to obtain its object. If I leave you as I found you, I am not God's channel. I am not here to entertain you, but to get you to the place where you can laugh at the impossible."[3]

If Bill Gaither's song "He Touched Me" were written earlier, Smith Wigglesworth's powerful voice no doubt would have rattled the windows of the meeting halls with that testimonial song. But he used other songs of his day that inspired people to believe. A friend and fellow minister in England, William Hacking, remembered Wigglesworth holding his little New Testament on the top of his head while he sang this refrain:

> I know the Lo-o-rd, I know the Lo-o-rd,
> I know the Lord has laid his hand on me.

After leading the congregation in the chorus several times, Wigglesworth urged them to raise their hands in prayer and worship. Hacking also remembered another favorite chorus:

> Yes, filled with God. Yes, filled with God.
> Pardoned and cleansed and filled with God.
> Yes, filled with God. Yes, filled with God.
> Emptied of self and filled with God.[4]

An American minister and historian, Carl Brumback, recalled attending Wigglesworth's meetings and singing that same chorus. "To be in one of his inspiring services," he wrote, "to sing with him, 'Yes, filled with God,' and to witness the miracle-working power of God was truly an unforgettable experience."[5]

But the most remembered Wigglesworth chorus was "Only Believe." Written by evangelist Paul Rader one night as he carried a sick child through his home, this simple yet powerful chorus rang from Wigglesworth's throat with more enthusiasm and volume than a cheerleading team could muster in a critical moment of a championship game.

Only believe, only believe;
All things are possible,
Only believe;

Only believe, only believe;
All things are possible,
Only believe.

Rader must have smiled if he ever heard the short, stocky preacher's unmistakable Yorkshire brogue when he sang "honly" for "only." And it is said that he would spell it out to the audience in typical Wigglesworth style: "h-o-n-e-l-y." Then he would call for the audience to change the lyrics into a personal testimony: "Lord, I believe. Lord, I believe. All things are possible. Lord, I believe." A converted boxer had written it, but a former plumber took it for his own. And at Wigglesworth's burial service, the mourners sang it in his memory.

Armed with the Word of God for his authority, an indomitable faith, an anointed and unique delivery—and bolstered with faith-building choruses—Smith Wigglesworth delivered his sermons around the world. But preaching was not an end in itself. To simply give a benediction after preaching would never happen in his meetings. The "Apostle of Faith" always expected signs and wonders to follow—with no less faith than that exhibited in the early church.

"Faith is the audacity that rejoices in the fact that God cannot break his own Word," Wigglesworth thundered. "Faith is not agitation. It is quiet confidence that God means what he says and we act on his Word."[6]

People who came to him for the laying on of hands knew that it would not be a gentle touch from the powerful hands that had grown calloused from wrestling heavy pipes and wrenches. If they had seen him in action in previous services, they would expect to hear his gruff question, "What's up?" In other words, "What is wrong with you?" If the sick person mentioned that he or she had stomach problems, it was not unusual for Wigglesworth to smack the person in the hurting area while he prayed and cast out the "demon." It was said that more than a few people changed their minds about telling Wigglesworth their real problems because of fear that he would strike that ailing organ or area.

Wigglesworth explained that his unusual treatment came as a result of his anger at the devil, that it was the devil he was hitting; the people just happened to be in the way. Ernest S. Williams, a Philadelphia pastor in the 1920s and later general superintendent of the Assemblies of God, told me he took his elders to Glad Tidings Tabernacle in New York to hear Wigglesworth preach. Thinking they might invite him to Philadelphia, Williams said the elders changed their minds when they saw how roughly he handled the sick.

In yet another Glad Tidings meeting, it was reported that Wigglesworth in his typical fashion struck an Irish immigrant woman who had come for prayer. She reacted quickly by drawing back her fist and shouting, "Begorra, if it's a fight you want, it's a fight you'll get!" Fortunately, cooler heads prevailed and the healing service continued in peace.

Despite occasional negative reactions such as these, followers from England to Australia and from Norway to North America accepted Smith Wigglesworth as he was. They viewed this former plumber as a twentieth-century apostle—or perhaps more definitively, a modern son of thunder.

It should be remembered too, as Donald Gee noted in the foreword, that Wigglesworth empathized more with those in his prayer lines after his own three-year battle with extremely painful gallstones. During his last crusade in San Francisco's Glad Tidings Temple in 1935, the church's magazine referred to him as "very lowly in spirit, and much more gentle and mellow."[7]

The many letters asking for his prayers would often bring this compassionate man to tears, and he would weep and pray before he answered. Unlike many who pray for the sick, Wigglesworth would inquire later about the condition of people for whom he had prayed. In his last conversation, while waiting for the start of a funeral service for an old friend, he asked the condition of a certain sick woman. The next moment he was with the Lord.

Eleven years earlier Wigglesworth had prophesied to South African David du Plessis that God would pour out his Spirit on mainline denominations—a move which would eclipse even what had happened during the previous thirty-six years in the pentecostal movement. "The Lord said to me," Wigglesworth explained to Du Plessis, "that I am to give you warning that he is going to use you in this movement. You will have a very important part."[8] Wigglesworth said he himself would not live to see it. Church history records that Du Plessis did indeed witness to thousands of people in the World Council of Churches and Roman Catholic settings, and helped prepare the way for the charismatic movement beginning in about 1960.

Wigglesworth's second prophecy on spiritual renewal came during a week-long campaign, the week before he died. "The first move [prophesied to Du Plessis] would bring the restoration of the gifts of the Spirit; the second would bring a revival of emphasis on the Word of God." And he added that when the two moves combined, "we shall see the greatest move the church of Jesus Christ has ever seen."[9] Millions believe they have seen the fulfillment of these two prophecies.

Now, before you read this collection of messages, pause to prepare yourself for simple yet powerful words from one of God's unique people. Smith Wigglesworth was living proof that daily walking and talking with God were not only possible but also essential in this spiritual warfare. You could use the following prayer as a way of inviting God to be at work in your own life.

Almighty God, I thank you for the anointed ministry of your servant, Smith Wigglesworth, and ask that as I meditate on these messages my faith will be challenged and increased. Help me to draw closer to you in my daily walk. Help me to believe you for [mention your own concerns] *and for the needs of my loved ones and community.*

As a believer, I am confident that in all things your grace is sufficient for me. Help me to share the gospel with others, always remembering that you love the world and that Jesus came to this earth to die for our sins, and that you will forgive our sins and strengthen us in our weaknesses. I ask that the Holy Spirit will help me to do my part in pointing others to the Savior. I ask these favors in the mighty name of Jesus Christ my Lord. Amen.

PART ONE:

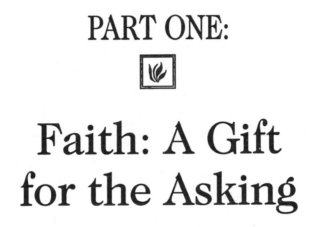

Faith: A Gift for the Asking

ONE

What Is Faith?

"Now faith is the substance of things hoped for, the evidence of things not seen. For by it the elders obtained a good report" (Hebrews 11:1-2). God has moved me tonight to speak on the marvelous, glorious reality of God's Word. How great should be our faith, for we cannot be saved except by faith; we cannot be kept but by faith; we can be baptized only by faith; and we will be caught up by faith. Therefore, what a blessed reality is faith in the living God.

What is faith? Faith is the very nature of God. It is the Word of God. It is the personal, inward flow of divine favor which moves in every fiber of our being until our whole nature is so quickened that we live by faith, we move by faith, and we are going to be caught up to glory by faith, for "faith is the victory!" Faith is the glorious knowledge of a personal presence within you, changing you from strength to strength, from glory to glory, until you get to the place where you walk with God, and where God thinks and speaks through you by the power of the Holy Ghost. Oh, it is grand, it is glorious!

God wants us to have far more than that which we can handle and see, and so he speaks of the substance of things hoped for, the evidence of things not seen. But, with the eye of faith, we may see it in all its beauty and grandeur. God's Word is from everlasting to everlasting, and "faith is the substance."

If I should give some of you ladies a piece of cloth, scissors, needle, and thread, you could produce a garment. Why? Because you would have the material. If I should provide some of you men with wood, saw, hammer, and nails, you could produce a box. Why? Because you would have the material. But God, without material, spoke the Word and produced this world with all its beauty. There was no material there, but the Word of God called it into being by his creative force.

Likewise, if you are begotten by this incorruptible Word, which lives and abides forever, you know that within you is this living, definite hope, greater than yourself, more powerful than any dynamic force in the world, for faith works in you by the power of the new creation of God in Christ Jesus.

Therefore, with the audacity of faith we should throw ourselves into the omnipotence of God's divine plan, for God has said, "All things *are* possible to him that believeth" (Mark 9:23). It is possible for the power of God to be so manifest in your human life that you will never be as you were before; for you will be ever going forward, from victory to victory, for faith knows no defeat.

GOD OPENS THE DOOR OF FAITH

The Word of God will bring you into a wonderful place of rest in faith. God intends that you have a clear conception of what faith is, how faith came, and how it remains. Faith is in the divine plan, for it brings you to the open door that you might enter in. You must have an open door, for you cannot open the door; it is God who does it, but he wants you to be ready to step in and claim his promises of all the divine manifestation of power in the name of Christ Jesus. It is only thus that you will be able to meet and conquer the enemy, for "greater is he that is in you, than he that is in the world" (1 John 4:4).

Living faith brings glorious power and personality. It gives divine ability, for it is by faith that Christ is manifested in your mortal flesh by the Word of God. I would not have you miss the knowledge that you have heard from God, and to realize that he has so changed you that all weakness, fear, inability—everything that has made you a failure—has passed away. Faith has the power to make you what God wants you to be; only you must be ready to step into the plan and believe his Word.

The first manifestation of God's plan was the cross of Calvary. You may refuse it; you may resist it. But God, who loves you with an everlasting love, has followed you through life, and will follow you with his great grace, that he may bring you to a knowledge of this great salvation.

God, in his own plan for your eternal good, may have brought something into your life which is distasteful, something that is causing you to feel desperate, to feel that your life is worthless. What does it mean? It means that the Spirit of God is showing you your own weakness so that you might cry out unto him. And when you do, he will show you the cross of redemption. Then God will give you faith to believe, for faith is the gift of God.

God, who has given us this faith, has a wonderful plan for our lives. Do you remember when God brought you to this place of salvation, how the faith he gave you brought a great desire to do something for him, and then he showed you that wonderful open door?

I was saved over sixty-seven years ago, and I have never lost the witness of the Spirit. If you will not allow your human nature to crush your faith and interfere with God's plan in its glorious divine setting, you will mount up like the eagles. Oh, the wonderful effectiveness of God's perfect plan working in us, with the divine Trinity flowing through humanity, changing our very nature to the extent that we cannot disbelieve, but act faith, talk faith, and in faith sing praises to the Lord. There is no room for anything that is "taught-faith," for God has brought us beyond the natural plane into a new atmosphere where he has enclosed us.

FAITH IS THE SUBSTANCE

Faith is an increasing position, always triumphant. It is not a place of poverty but of wealth. If you always live in fruitfulness, you will always have plenty. What does it say in this verse? "The elders obtained a good report" (Hebrews 11:2). The person who lives in faith always has a good report. The Acts of the Apostles were written because the lives of the apostles bore the fruit of active faith. To them faith was an everyday fact. If your life is in the divine order, you will not only have living, active faith but you will always be building up someone else in faith.

What is the good of preaching without faith? God intends that we should so live in this glorious sphere of the power of God that we will always be in a position to tell people of the *act* that brought the *fact*. Indeed, you must *act* before you can see the *fact*. What is the good of praying for the sick without faith? You must believe that God will not deny himself, for the Word of God cannot be denied. I believe this message is given in divine order, that you may no longer be in a place of doubt, but will realize that "faith is the substance!" (Hebrews 11:1a).

Beloved, even with all the faith we have, we are not even so much as touching the hem of God's plan for us. It is like going to the seashore and dipping your toe into the water, with the great, vast ocean before you. God wants us to rise on the bosom of the tide and quit paddling along the shore. Oh, to be connected with the sublime power, that human nature may know God and the glory of the manifestation of Christ!

The Word of God is eternal and cannot be broken. You cannot improve on the Word of God, for it is life and it produces life. Listen! God has begotten you to a "lively hope" (1 Peter 1:3). You are begotten of the Word that created worlds. If you dare to believe, it is powerful. God wants us to be powerful, a people of faith, a purified people, a people who will launch out in God and dare to trust him in glorious faith which always takes us beyond that which is commonplace to an abiding place in God.

THE MAN AND HIS MESSAGE

Originally titled "A Living Faith" from *Glad Tidings Herald* (New York City), February 1935, page 1, a newspaper published by Glad Tidings Tabernacle (Assemblies of God), still located just a block from Madison Square Garden.

"If a thing is in the Bible," Wigglesworth would say, "it is so; it is not even to be prayed about; it is to be received and acted upon. Inactivity of faith is a robber which steals blessing. Increase comes by action, by using what we have and what we know. Your life must be one of going from faith to faith."[1]

TWO

The Door to Life Eternal

Hebrews 11, the "faith chapter," is a wonderful passage. In fact, all of the Word of God is wonderful. It is not only wonderful, but it also holds the power to change conditions. Any natural condition can be changed by the Word of God, which is a supernatural power.

In the Word of God is the breath, the nature, and the power of the living God, and his power works in every person who dares to believe his Word. There is life through the power of it. And as we receive the Word in faith, we receive the nature of God himself. It is as we lay hold of God's promises in simple faith that we become partakers of the divine nature into grace, a power that makes dead things live, and a power which is of God, which will be manifested in our flesh.

This power has come forth with its glory to transform us by divine act into sons of God, to make us like unto the Son of God, by the Spirit of God who moves us on from grace to grace and from glory to glory as our faith rests in this living Word.

It is important that we have a foundational truth, something greater than ourselves upon which to rest. In Hebrews 12 we read, "Looking unto Jesus the author and finisher of *our* faith" (vs 2). Jesus is our life and he is the power of our life. We see in the fifth chapter of Acts that as soon as Peter was let out of prison, he heard the Lord say to him, "Go... speak... all the words of this life" (vs 20). There is only one Book that has life. In this Word we find him who came that we might have life and have it more abundantly, and by faith this life is imparted to us.

When we come into this life by divine faith (and we must realize that it is by grace we are saved through faith, and that it is not of ourselves, but is the gift of God), we become partakers of this life. This Word is greater than anything else. There is no darkness in it at all.

Those who dwell in this Word are able under all circumstances to say that they are willing to come to the light that their deeds may be made manifest. Outside of this Word is darkness, and the people of darkness do not want to come to the light because their deeds are evil. But the moment we are saved by the power of the Word of God, we love the light, we love the truth. The inexpressible divine power, force, passion, and fire that we receive is of God. Drink, my beloved, drink deeply of this source of life.

MORE REAL THAN WHAT YOU CAN SEE AND TOUCH

Faith is the substance of things hoped for. Someone said to me one day, "I would not believe in anything I could not handle and see." Everything you can handle and see is temporary and will perish with the using. But the things not seen are eternal and will not fade away. Are you dealing with tangible things or with the things which are eternal, the things that are facts, that are made real by faith?

Thank God that through the knowledge of the truth of the Son of God, I have within me a greater power, a mightier working, an inward impact of life, of power, of vision, and of truth more real than anyone can know who lives in the realm of the tangible. God manifests himself to the person who dares to believe.

But there is something more beautiful than that. When we receive divine life in the new birth, we receive a nature that delights to do the will of God. As we believe the Word of God, a well of water springs up within our hearts. A spring is always better than a pump, but I know that even a spring is apt to be outclassed when we receive the baptism of the Holy Ghost. It was a spring to the woman at the well, but with the person who has the Holy Ghost, it is flowing rivers.

Have you these flowing rivers? To be filled with the Holy Ghost is to be filled with the Executive of the Godhead, who brings to us all the Father has and all the Son desires. And we should live so in the Spirit that God can cause us to move with his authority and reign by his divine ability.

I thank God he baptizes with the Holy Ghost. I know he did it for me because they heard me speak in tongues and then I heard myself. That was a scriptural work and I don't want anything else, because I must be an epistle of God. There must be emanating through my body a whole epistle of the life, of the power, and of the resurrection of my Lord Jesus. Wonderful things happen through this divine union with God himself.

Listen to these words: "God . . hath in these last days spoken unto us by *his* Son, whom he hath appointed heir of all things, by whom also he made the worlds" (Hebrews 1:1-2). By this divine Person, this Word, this Son, God made all things. Notice that it says that he made the worlds by this Person, and you know that he made them out of the things that were not there.

Everything we see was made by this divine Son. I want you to see that as you receive the Son of God, and as Christ dwells in your heart by faith, there is within you a divine force, the power of limitless possibilities. And that as a result of this incoming

Christ, God wants to do great things through you. By faith, if we receive and accept his Son, God brings us into sonship, and not only into sonship but into joint-heirship, into sharing together with him all that the Son possesses.

I am more and more convinced every day I live that very few who are saved by the grace of God have a right conception of how great is their authority over darkness, demons, death, and every power of the enemy. It is a real joy when we realize our inheritance along this line.

I was speaking like this one day and one man said, "I have never heard anything like this before. How many months did it take you to get up that sermon?"

I answered, "My brother, God pressed my wife from time to time to get me to preach, and I promised her I would preach. I used to labor hard for a week to get something up, then give out the text and sit down and say, 'I am done.' Oh, brother, I have given up getting things *up*. They all come *down*. And the sermons that come down stop down, then go back up, because the Word of God says his Word shall not return unto him void. But if *I* get anything up, it will not stay up very long, and when it goes down, it will take me with it."

FILLED TO OVERFLOWING

The sons and daughters of God are made manifest in this present day to destroy the power of the devil. To be saved by the power of God is to be brought from the realm of the ordinary into the extraordinary, from the natural into the divine. Do you remember the day when the Lord laid his hands on you? You say, "I could not do anything but praise the Lord." Well, that was only the beginning. Where are you today? The divine plan is that you increase until you receive the measureless fulness of God.

You do not have to say, "I tell you it was wonderful when I

was baptized with the Holy Ghost." If you have to look back to the past to make me know you are baptized, then you are backslidden. If the beginning was good, it ought to be better day by day, till everybody is fully convinced that you are filled with the might of God in the Spirit. Filled with all the fulness of God!

"Be not drunk with wine, wherein is excess; but be filled with the Spirit" (Ephesians 5:18). I don't want anything else than being full, and fuller, and fuller, until I am overflowing like a great, big vat. Do you realize that if you have been created anew and begotten again by the Word of God, there is within you the Word of power and the same light and life as the Son of God himself had?

God wants to flow through you with measureless power of divine utterance and grace till your whole body is a flame of fire. God intends each soul touched by Pentecost to be a live wire— not a *monument,* but a *movement.* So many people have been baptized with the Holy Ghost. There was a movement, but they have become monuments and you cannot move them!

God wake us out of sleep lest we should become indifferent to the glorious truth and the breath of the almighty power of God. We must be the light and salt of the earth, with the whole armor of God upon us. It would be a serious thing if enemies were about and we had to go back and fetch our sandals. It would be a serious thing if we had on no breastplate. How can you be furnished with the armor? Take it by faith. Jump in, stop in, and never come out, for this is a baptism to be lost in, where you only know one thing and that is the desire of God at all times. The baptism in the Spirit should be an ever increasing endowment of power, an ever increasing enlargement of grace.

O, Father, grant unto us a real look into the glorious liberty you have designed for the children of God, those who are delivered from this present world, separated, sanctified, and made suitable for your use, and whom you have designed to be filled with all your fulness.

THE FIGHT OF FAITH

Nothing has hurt me so much as this, to see so-called believers have so much unbelief in them that it is hard to move them. There is no difficulty in praying for a sinner to be healed. But when you touch a believer, he comes back and says, "You did not pray for my legs."

I say you are healed all over if you believe. Everything is possible to those who believe. God will not fail his Word whatever you are. Suppose that all the people in the world did not believe. That would make no difference to God's Word; it would be the same. You cannot alter God's Word. It is from everlasting to everlasting, and those who believe in it shall be like Mount Zion which cannot be moved.

I was preaching on faith one time and there was in the audience a man who said three times, "I won't believe." I kept right on preaching because that made no difference to me. I am prepared for a fight any day, for the fight of faith, that is. We must keep the faith which has been committed to us. I went on preaching and the man shouted out, "I won't believe." As he passed out of the door, he cried out again, "I won't believe."

The next day a message came saying that as soon as that man left the meeting, the Spirit said to him, "Because you would not believe, you shall be dumb." It was the same Spirit who came to Zechariah and said, "Thou shalt be dumb, and not able to speak, until the day that these things shall be performed, because thou believest not my words" (Luke 1:20). I believe in a hell. Who is in hell? The unbeliever. If you want to go to hell, all you need to do is to reject the Word of God. The unbelievers are there.

I said to the leader of the meeting where the man was struck dumb, "You go and see this man and find out if these reports are true." He went to the house and the first to greet him was the man's wife. The leader inquired, "Is it true that your husband three times in the meeting declared that he would not believe, and now he cannot speak?" The woman burst into tears and said, "Go and see." The meeting leader went into the room and saw the man's mouth in a terrible state. The unbeliever got a piece of paper and wrote, "I had an opportunity to believe. I refused to believe, and now I cannot believe and I cannot speak."

The greatest sin in the world is to disbelieve God's Word. We are not of those who draw back, but we are of those who believe, for God's Word is a living Word and it always acts.

One day a stylishly dressed woman came to our meeting and walked up to the platform. Under her arm, going down underneath her dress, was a concealed crutch that nobody could see. She had been helpless in one leg for twenty years, had heard of what God was doing, and wanted us to pray for her. As soon as we did she exclaimed, "What have you done with my leg?" Three times she said it, and then we saw that the crutch was loose and hanging, and that she was standing straight.

The woman who was interpreting for me said to her, "We have done nothing with your leg. If anything has been done, it is God who has done it." She answered, "I have been lame and used a crutch for twenty years, but my leg is perfect now." We did not suggest that she kneel down at the altar, but thank God, she fell down among the others and cried for mercy.

I find that when God touches us, it is a divine touch of life power, and it thrills and quickens the body so that people know it is God, and conviction comes, and they cry for mercy. Praise God for anything that brings people to the throne of grace.

THE MOST IMPORTANT THING

God heals by the power of his Word. But here is the most important thing: are you saved, do you know the Lord, are you prepared to meet God? You may be an invalid as long as you live, but you may be saved by the power of God. You may have a strong, healthy body, but go straight to hell because you know nothing of the grace of God and salvation. Thank God I was saved in a moment, the moment I believed, and God will do the same for you.

God means by this divine power within you to make you follow after the mind of the Spirit by the Word of God, till you are entirely changed by the power of it. You might come onto this platform and say, "Wigglesworth, do you need anything from God for your body?" I will say now that I have a body in perfect condition and have nothing to ask for, and I am sixty-five years old.

It was not always so. This body was a frail, helpless body, but God fulfilled his Word to me according to Isaiah and Matthew. He himself took my infirmities and my diseases, my sicknesses, and by his stripes I am healed. It is fine to go up and down and not know you have a body. He took our infirmities, he bore our sicknesses, he came to heal our broken hearts.[1]

Jesus would have us come forth in divine likeness, in resurrection force, in the power of the Spirit, to walk in faith and understand his Word, what he meant when he said he would give us power over all the power of the enemy. Christ will subdue all things till everything comes into perfect harmony with his will.

Is he reigning over your affections, desires, and will? If so, you will be subject to his reigning power. He will be the authority over the whole situation. When God reigns, everything must be subservient to his divine plan and will for us.

See what the Word of God says: "No man can say that Jesus is the Lord, but by the Holy Ghost" (1 Corinthians 12:3b). "Lord!" Bless God forever. Oh, for him to be Lord and Master! For him to rule and control! For him to be filling your whole body with the plan of truth! Because you are in Christ Jesus, all things are subject to him. It is lovely, and God wants to make it so for you. When you get there you will find divine power continually working. I absolutely believe that none of us comes into the place of revelation and activity of the gifts of the Spirit but by this fulfilled promise of Jesus that he will baptize us in the Holy Ghost.

FAITH IN ACTION

I was taken to see a beautiful, nine-year-old boy who was lying on a bed. The mother and father were distracted because he had been lying there for seven months. They had to lift and feed him. The boy was like a statue with flashing eyes. As soon as I entered the place, the Lord revealed to me the cause of the trouble. So I said to the mother, "The Lord shows me there is something wrong with his stomach."

She said, "Oh, no, we have had two physicians and they say it is paralysis of the mind." I said, "God reveals to me it is his stomach." "Oh, no, it isn't. These physicians ought to know. They have x-rayed him."

The gentleman who brought me there said to the mother, "You have sent for this man, you have been the means of his coming, now don't you stand against him. This man knows what he has got to do." But Dr. Jesus knows more than that. He knows everything. All you have to do is ring your bell for Jesus and he will come down.

Who shall interfere with the divine mind of the Spirit which has all revelation, who understands the whole condition of life? For the Word of God declares he knows all things and is well acquainted with the manifestation of our bodies, for everything is naked and open before him. Having the mind of the Spirit, we understand what is the will of God.

Having that confidence, I prayed over the boy and laid my hands on his stomach. He became sick and vomited a worm thirteen inches long, and was perfectly restored. Who knows? God knows.

When shall we come into the knowledge of God? When we cease from our own minds and allow ourselves to become clothed with the mind and authority of Almighty God.

The Spirit of God would have us understand that nothing can interfere with our coming into perfect blessing except unbelief. Unbelief is a terrible hindrance. As soon as we are willing to allow the Holy Ghost to have his way, we will find great things will happen all the time. But, oh, how much of our own human reason we have to get rid of, how much human planning we have to become divorced from. What would happen right now if everybody believed God? I love the thought that God the Holy Ghost wants to emphasize that truth. If we will only yield ourselves to the divine plan, he is right there to bring forth the mystery of truth.

How many of us believe the Word? It is easy to quote it, but it is more important to have it than to quote it. It is very easy for me to quote, "Now are we the sons of God" (1 John 3:2a), but it is more important for me to know whether I *am* a son of God. When the Son was on the earth, he was recognized by the people who heard him. Never had a man spoken like him. His word carried power, and that word came to pass.

Sometimes you quote, "Greater is he that is in you, than he that is in the world" (1 John 4:4b), and you could tell just where to find it. But, beloved, is it so? Can demons remain in your presence? You have to be greater than demons. Can disease lodge in the body that you touch? You have to be greater than the disease. Can anything in the world stand against you and hold its place if it is indeed a fact that greater is he who is in you than he who is in the world? Dare we stand on the line with the Word of God and face the facts of the difficulties before us?

FROM DEATH TO LIFE

I can never forget the face of a former policeman in Switzerland who came to me one time. His clothes hung from him, his whole frame was shriveled, his eyes were glaring and glassy, his jawbones stuck out, his whole being was a manifestation of death. He said to me, "Can you help me?"

Could I help him? Just as we believe the Word of God can we help anybody, but we must be sure we are firmly standing on the Word of God. If we are on the Word of God, it must take place. As I looked at this man I thought I had never seen anybody alive that looked like him. I said, "What is it?"

He answered with a breathless voice, "I had a cancer on my chest. I was operated on and in removing the cancer, they removed my swallower; so now I can breathe but cannot swallow." The emaciated man pulled out a tube about nine inches long with a cup at the top and an opening at the bottom which fitted into a hole. He showed me that he pressed one part of the tube into his stomach and poured liquid into the top, and for three months had been keeping himself alive that way. It was a living death.

Could I help him? See what the Word of God says: "Whosoever... shall not doubt in his heart, but shall believe that those things which he saith shall come to pass; he shall have whatsoever he saith" (Mark 11:23). God wants to move us along scriptural lines.

On those lines I said, "You shall have a good supper tonight." "But," he said, "I cannot swallow." I said, "You shall have a good supper tonight." "But I cannot swallow." "You shall have a good supper; go and eat."

When he got home he told his wife that the preacher had said he would have a good supper that night. "If you will get something ready, I'll see if I can swallow." His wife got a good supper ready and he took a mouthful. He had taken mouthfuls before but they would not go down. But the Word of God said "whatsoever," and this mouthful went down, and more and more went down until he was full.

Then what happened? He went to bed with the joy of the knowledge that he could again swallow, and he wakened the next morning with that same joy. He looked for a hole in his stomach, but God had closed that hole when he opened the other. Wherever he went, people came out and said, "Let us go and look at him." He said, "I am just full to overflowing with praises to God for the faith that works impossibilities."

Faith is the substance of things hoped for. Faith is the Word. You were begotten of the Word, the Word is in you, the life of the Son is in you, and God wants you to believe.

THE MAN AND HIS MESSAGE

Originally titled "The Substance of Things Hoped For" from the *Pentecostal Evangel* (Springfield, Missouri), October 25, 1924, pages 2-4.

A note along with this printed sermon stated that Wigglesworth's new book, *Ever-Increasing Faith*, had sold twenty-five hundred copies during the previous ten weeks. Editor Carrie Judd Montgomery apologized in her *Triumphs of Faith* (December 1924) that she was unable to fill the many orders for the book because the first two printings were already exhausted.

It is not surprising to learn that other ministers, seeing Wigglesworth's popularity and success, would copy his preaching style and mannerisms. In one such incident George Stormont reported that students at a San Francisco Bible school (probably Glad Tidings) noticed that Wigglesworth stroked his mustache while he preached. "After he left, many of the students [who had no mustaches] when preaching could be seen stroking 'the substance of things hoped for, the evidence of things not seen'!"[2]

THREE

❧

Awake to Take!

In Romans 4:16 we read, "*It is* of faith, that *it might be* by grace"; meaning that we can open the door and God will come in. What will happen if we really open the door by faith? God is greater than our thoughts. He puts it to us: "Exceeding abundantly above all that we ask or think" (Ephesians 3:20b). When we ask a lot, God says "more." Are we ready for the "more"? And then the "much more"? If we are not ready, we may miss it.

We can be so endued by the Spirit of the Lord in the morning that it shall be a tonic for the whole day. God can so thrill us with new life that nothing ordinary or small will satisfy us after that. There is a great place for us in God where we won't be satisfied with small things. We won't have any satisfaction unless the fire falls, and whenever we pray we will have the assurance that what we have prayed for is going to follow the moment we open our mouths. Oh, this praying in the Spirit! This great plan of God for us! In a moment we can go right in. In where? Into his will. Then all things will be well.

You can't receive anything if you are asleep. The world is always awake, and we should always be awake to what God has for us. Awake to take! Awake to hold it after we get it! How much can you take? We know that God is more willing to give than we are to receive. How shall we dare sleep when the Spirit commands us to take everything on the table. It is the greatest banquet that ever was and ever will be—the table where all you take only leaves more behind. A fulness that cannot be exhausted! Are you prepared for a lot?

THE FRUIT OF FAITH

Let us take a look at this wonderful Word of God: "And Jesus entered into Jerusalem, and into the temple: and when he had looked round about upon all things, and now the eventide was come, he went out unto Bethany with the twelve. And on the morrow, when they were come from Bethany, he was hungry. And seeing a fig tree afar off having leaves, he came, if haply he might find any thing thereon: and when he came to it, he found nothing but leaves; for the time of figs was not yet. And Jesus answered and said unto it, 'No man eat fruit of thee hereafter for ever.' And his disciples heard it" (Mark 11:11-14).

Jesus was sent from God to meet the world's need. Jesus lived to minister life by the words he spoke. He said to Philip, "He that hath seen me hath seen the Father... the words that I speak unto you, I speak not of myself: but the Father that dwelleth in me" (John 14:9-10). I am persuaded that if we are filled with his words of life and the Holy Ghost, and Christ is made manifest in our mortal flesh, then the Holy Ghost can really move us with his life, his words, till as he was, so are we in the world. We are receiving our life from God, and it is always kept in tremendous activity, working in our whole nature as we live in perfect contact with God.

Jesus spoke, and everything he said must come to pass. That is the great plan. When we are filled only with the Holy Spirit, and we won't allow the Word of God to be detracted from by what we hear or by what we read, then comes the inspiration, then the life, then the activity, then the glory! Oh, to live in it! To live in it is to be moved by it. To live in it is to be moved so that we will have God's life, God's personality in the human body.

By the grace of God I want to impart the Word, and bring you into a place where you will dare to act upon the plan of the Word, to so breathe life by the power of the Word that it is impossible for you to go on under any circumstances without his provision. The most difficult things that come to us are to our advantage from God's side. When we come to the place of impossibilities, it is the grandest place for us to see the possibilities of God.

Put this right in your mind and never forget it: you will never be of any importance to God till you venture into the impossible. God wants people on the daring line. I do not mean foolish daring. "Be filled with the Spirit" (Ephesians 5:18b), and when we are filled with the Spirit, we are not so much concerned about the secondary thing. It is the first with God.

Everything evil, everything unclean, everything satanic in any way is an objectionable thing to God, and we are to live above it, destroy it, not allow it to have any place. Jesus didn't let the devil answer back. We must reach the place where we will not allow anything to interfere with the plan of God.

Jesus and his disciples came to the tree. It looked beautiful. It had the appearance of fruit, but when he came to it, Jesus found nothing but leaves. He was very disappointed. Looking at the tree, he spoke to it. Here is shown forth his destructive power, "No man eat fruit of thee hereafter forever" (Mark 11:14).

The next day they were passing by the same way and the disciples saw the tree "dried up from the roots" (Mark 11:20b). They said to Jesus, "Behold, the fig tree which thou cursedst is withered away" (vs 21). And Jesus said, "Have faith in God" (vs 22). There isn't a person who has ever seen a tree dried from the *root*. Trees always show the first signs of death right at the top. But the Master had spoken. The Master dealt with a natural thing to reveal to these disciples a supernatural plan. If he spoke, the tree would have to obey.

PUTTING GOD FIRST

God, the Holy Ghost, wants us to understand clearly that we are the mouthpiece of God and are here for his divine plan. We may allow the natural mind to dethrone his lordship, but in the measure we do, we won't come into the treasure which God has for us. The Word of God must have first place. It must not have a second place. In any measure that we doubt the Word of God, from that moment we have ceased to thrive spiritually and actively. The Word of God is not only to be looked at and read, but received as the Word of God to become life right within our life. "Thy word have I hid in mine heart, that I might not sin against thee" (Psalm 119:11).

"I give unto you power... over all the power of the enemy" (Luke 10:19). There it is. We can accept or reject it. I accept and believe it. It is a word beyond all human calculation. "Have faith in God" (Mark 11:22). These disciples were in the Master's school. They were the men who were to turn the world upside down. As we receive the Word we will never be the same. If we dare to act as the Word goes forth and not be afraid, then God will honor us. "The Lord of hosts *is* with us; the God of Jacob *is* our refuge" (Psalm 46:7). Jacob was the weakest of all, in any way you like to take it. He is the God of Jacob, and he is our God. So we may likewise have our names changed to Israel.

As the Lord Jesus injected this wonderful word, "Have faith in God," into the disciples, he began to show how it was to be. Looking around about, Jesus saw the mountains, and he began to make a practical application. A truth means nothing unless it moves us. We can have our *minds* filled a thousand times, but it must get into our *hearts* if there are to be any results. All inspiration is in the heart. All compassion is in the heart.

Looking at the mountains Jesus said, "[He who] shall not doubt in his heart" (Mark 11:23). That is the barometer. You know exactly where you are. You know when you pray. If your heart is right, how it leaps. No one is any good for God and never makes progress in God who does not hate sin. You are never safe. But there is a place in God where you can love righteousness and where you can hate iniquity till the Word of God is a light in your bosom, quickening every fiber of your body, thrilling your whole nature. The pure in heart see God. Believe in the heart! What a word! If I believe in my heart, God says I can begin to speak, and "whatsoever" I say shall come to pass.

Here is an act of believing in the heart. I was called to Halifax, England, to pray for a woman missionary. It was an urgent call as I could see there was an absence of faith, and I could see there was death. Death is a terrible thing, and God wants to keep us alive. I know it is appointed unto us once to die, but I believe in a rapturous death.

I said to the woman, "How are you?" She said, "I have faith," in a very weak tone of voice. "Faith? Why you are dying? Brother Walshaw, is she dying?" "Yes." "Nurse, is she dying?" "Yes." Of a friend standing by, I asked again, "Is she dying?" "Yes."

Now I believe there is something in a heart that is against defeat, and this is the faith which God has given to us. I said to her, "In the name of Jesus, now believe and you'll live." The woman said, "I believe," and God sent life from her head to her feet. They dressed her and she lived.

FAITH IS GOD IN THE HUMAN VESSEL

"Have faith." It isn't saying you must stir up faith. Faith is God in the human vessel, in the one who *believes in his heart*. It is a grasping of the eternal God. "This is the victory that overcometh the world, *even* our faith" (1 John 5:4b). He who believes overcomes the world. "Faith *cometh* by hearing, and

hearing by the Word of God" (Romans 10:17). He who believes
in his heart! Can you imagine anything easier than that? He who
believes in his heart!

What is the process by which this comes to pass? Death! No
one can remain alive who believes in his heart. He dies to everything worldly. He who loves the world is not of God. You can
measure the whole thing and examine yourself to see if you
have faith. Faith is a life. Faith enables you to lay hold of that
which is and get it out of the way for God to bring in something that is not.

Recently, when I was in Norway, a woman wrote to me from
England saying she had been operated on for cancer three years
before but that it was now coming back. She was living in constant dread of the whole thing as the operation had been so
painful. Would it be possible for her to see me when I returned
to England? I wrote that I would be passing through London
on the twentieth of June that year. If she would like to meet me,
I would pray for her. She agreed to meet me.

When I met the woman I saw she was in great pain, and I
have great sympathy for people who have tried to get relief and
have failed. (If you preachers lose your compassion, you can stop
preaching, for it won't do any good. You will only be successful
as a preacher as you let your heart become filled with the compassion of Jesus.) As soon as I saw her I entered into the state of
her mind. I saw how distressed she was. She came to me in a
mournful spirit, and her whole face was downcast.

I said to her, "There are two things going to happen today.
One is that you are to know that you are saved." "Oh, if I could
only know I was saved," she said. "There is another thing. You
have to go out of this hotel without any pain, without a trace of
the cancer."

Then I began with the Word. Oh, this wonderful Word! We
do not have to go up to bring God down; neither do we have to
go down to bring him up. "The word is nigh thee, *even* in thy
mouth, and in thy heart: that is, the word of faith, which we

preach" (Romans 10:8). I said to her, "Believe that Jesus Christ took your sins when he died at the cross. Believe that when he was buried, it was for you. Believe that when he arose, it was for you. And now at God's right hand he is sitting for you. If you can believe in your heart and confess with your mouth, you shall be saved."

The woman looked at me saying, "Oh, it is going all through my body. I know I am saved now. If he comes today, I'll go. How I have dreaded the thought of his coming all my life! But if he comes today, I know I shall be ready." The first thing was finished. Now for the second. I laid my hands upon her in the name of Jesus, believing in my heart that I could say what I wanted and it should be done. I said, "In the name of Jesus, I cast this out." The woman jumped up. "Two things have happened," she said. "I am saved and now the cancer is gone."

Faith will stand amid the wrecks of time,
Faith unto eternal glories climb;
Only count the promise true,
And the Lord will stand by you—
Faith will win the victory *every time!*

THE DOSE THAT CURES

So many people have nervous trouble. I'll tell you how to get rid of your nervous trouble. I have something in my bag, one dose of which will cure you: "I *am* the Lord that healeth thee" (Exodus 15:26b). How this wonderful Word of God changes the situation. "There is no fear in love; but perfect love casteth out fear" (1 John 4:18a). I have tested that truth so often, casting out the whole condition of fear and seeing the whole situation changed. We have a big God, but we must absolutely trust him. The people who really do believe God are strong, and "he that hath clean hands shall be stronger and stronger" (Job 17:9b).

At the close of a certain meeting a man said to me, "You have helped everybody but me. I wish you would help me." I asked, "What's the trouble with you?" He answered, "I cannot sleep because of nervous trouble. My wife says she has not known me to have a full night's sleep for three years. I am just shattered." Anybody could tell he was.

I put my hands upon him and said, "Brother, I believe in my heart. Go home and sleep in the name of Jesus." "I can't sleep," he answered. "Go home and sleep in the name of Jesus." And he said again, "I can't sleep." The lights were being put out, and I took the man by the coat collar and said, "Don't talk to me anymore." That was sufficient. He left after that.

When he got home his mother and wife said to him, "What has happened?" "Nothing. He helped everybody but me." "Surely he said something to you." "He told me to come home and sleep in the name of Jesus, but you know I can't sleep in *anything*." His wife urged him to do what I had said, and he had scarcely put his head on the pillow before the Lord put him to sleep.

The next morning the man was still asleep. And the next morning he was still asleep. His wife began to make noise in the bedroom to awaken him, but he did not waken. Sunday morning he was still asleep. His wife decided to make a good Sunday dinner, and then awaken him. After the dinner was prepared she went up to her husband and put her hand on his shoulder and shook him, saying, "Are you never going to wake up?" From that night on that man never had any more nervousness.

A man came to me for whom I prayed. Then I asked, "Are you sure you are perfectly healed?" "Well," he said, "there is just a little pain in my shoulder." "Do you know what that is?" I asked him. "That is unbelief. Were you saved before you believed or after?" "After," he answered. "You will be healed after." "It is all right now," he said. It was all right before, but he hadn't believed. The Word of God is for each one of us. It is by faith that it might be by grace.

THE MAN AND HIS MESSAGE

Originally titled "The Way of Faith" from the *Pentecostal Evangel* (Springfield, Missouri), June 15, 1935, pages 2-3. On this tour of the United States during the Great Depression, Wigglesworth was seventy-six but still going strong.

An appreciative Anglican vicar, W.H. Stuart-Fox, whose son had been healed through Wigglesworth's ministry, invited the evangelist to preach in a tent set up near St. Saviour's Church, North London, in 1928. The British Assemblies of God magazine published the vicar's enthusiastic report. "That stalwart of evangelism which sets forth Christ as an all-sufficient Saviour for every need of body as well as soul, Mr. Smith Wigglesworth, spent ten busy days at St. Saviour's Church. The great truths so faithfully proclaimed of a full redemption for body, soul, and spirit through the atonement came with extraordinary freshness to the hungry crowds which day by day filled the tent till it overflowed. One of the striking features of the mission was the large number of men, old and young, which came forward to confess Christ, while there were many cases of healing."[1]

FOUR

Knowing God: The Key to Faith

I am reading from John's Gospel, chapter six, where the disciples asked Jesus an important question: "Then said they unto him, 'What shall we do, that we might work the works of God?' Jesus answered and said unto them, 'This is the work of God, that ye believe on him whom he hath sent'" (vs 28-29).

"This is the work of God, that you believe." Nothing in the world glorifies God so much as the simple rest of faith in what God's Word says. Jesus said, "My Father worketh hitherto, and I work" (John 5:17). He saw the way the Father did the works; it was on the groundwork of knowledge, faith based upon knowledge. When I know him, there are any amount of promises I can lay hold of. Then there is no struggle, "for every one that asketh receiveth; and he that seeketh findeth; and to him that knocketh it shall be opened" (Matthew 7:8).

Jesus lived to manifest God's glory on the earth, to show forth what his Father was like, that many sons might be brought to glory (Hebrews 2:10). John the Baptist came as a forerunner, testifying beforehand to the coming revelation of the Son. The

Son came, and in the power of the Holy Ghost revealed faith. The living God has chosen us in the midst of his people. The power is not of us, but of God. Yes, beloved, it is the power of another within us.

Just in the measure we are clothed and covered and hidden in him is his inner working manifested in us. Jesus said, "The works that I do shall [you] do also" (John 14:12); and "My Father worketh hitherto, and I work" (John 5:17). Oh, the joy of the knowledge of it! To know him. As we look back, we see how God has brought us through in his love and we can shout "hallelujah." When pressed beyond measure by the Spirit, God brings us face-to-face with reality. I must know the sovereignty of his grace and the manifestation of his power—his blessed Holy Spirit dwelling in me and manifesting his works.

Where am I? I am in Christ; he is in God, and in the Holy Ghost, the great revealer of the Son. Three persons dwelling in humankind. "Therefore be it known unto you that he who dwells in God does the works." "The law of the Spirit of life in Christ Jesus hath made me free from the law of sin and death" (Romans 8:2).

The Spirit works in righteousness, bringing us to the place where all unbelief is dethroned and Christ is made the head of the corner. "This is the Lord's doing, and it is marvelous in our eyes" (Matthew 21:42b). Here is a glorious fact: we are in God's presence, possessed by him; we are not our own, we are clothed with another. What for? For the deliverance of the people.

DARE TO BELIEVE

Many can testify to the day and hour when they were delivered from sickness by a supernatural power. Some would have passed away with influenza if God had not intervened.[1] But God stepped in with a new revelation, showing us that we are born from above, born by a new power, God dwelling in us and superseding the old. "If ye shall ask any thing in my name, I will do *it*" (John 14:14). Ask and receive, and your joy shall be full, if you dare to believe. God is more anxious to answer than we are to ask. I am speaking of faith based upon knowledge.

I was healed of appendicitis, and that because of faith based upon knowledge of that experience. Where I have ministered to others, God has met and answered according to his will. It is in our trust and knowledge that God will not fail us if we will only believe. The centurion told Jesus, "Speak the word only, and my servant shall be healed." Jesus said unto the centurion, "Go thy way; and as thou hast believed, *so* be it done unto thee. And his servant was healed in the selfsame hour" (Matthew 8:8, 13).

In one place where I was staying, a young man came in telling us that his sweetheart was dying, that there was no hope. I said, "Only believe." What was it? Faith based upon knowledge. I knew that what God had done for me he could do for her. We went to the house. Her sufferings were terrible to witness. I said, "In the name of Jesus come out of her."

The girl cried, "Mother, mother, I am well." Then I said that the only way to make us believe was for her to get up and dress. Presently she came down dressed. The doctor came in and examined her carefully. He said, "This is of God; this is the finger of God." It was faith based upon knowledge.

If I received a check for one thousand dollars and knew only imperfectly the character of the person who sent it, I should be careful not to count on it until it was honored. Jesus did great works because of his knowledge of his Father. Faith begets knowledge, fellowship, communion. If you see imperfect faith, full of doubt, a wavering condition, it always comes of imperfect knowledge.

Jesus said to his Father, "'I knew that thou hearest me always: but because of the people which stand by I said *it*, that they may believe that thou hast sent me'.... He cried with a loud voice, 'Lazarus, come forth'" (John 11:42-43). Consider Paul when he believed God: "And God wrought special miracles by the hands of Paul: So that from his body were brought unto the sick handkerchiefs or aprons, and the diseases departed from them, and the evil spirits went out of them" (Acts 19:11-12).

THE LATEST NEWS FROM THE GODHEAD

I thank God that he has cared for me these twelve years [after beginning to preach in 1907] and blessed me—giving me such a sense of his presence! When we depend upon God, how bountiful he is, giving us enough and to spare for others. Lately God has enabled me to win victory on new lines, a living, Holy Ghost attitude in a new way. As we meet, immediately the glory falls. The Holy Ghost has the latest news from the Godhead, and has designed for us the right place at the right time. Events happen in a remarkable way. You drop in right where the need is.

Recently I have faced several mental cases. How difficult they are naturally, but how easy for God to handle. One lady came, saying, "Just over the way there is a young man terribly afflicted, demented, with no rest day or night." I went with a very imperfect knowledge as to what I had to do, but in the weak places God helps our infirmities. I rebuked the demon in the name of Jesus. Then I said, "I'll come again tomorrow." The next day when I returned to the house, he was with his father in the field and quite well.

In another case fifty miles away, there was a fine young man, twenty-five years of age. He had lost his reason; he could have no communication with his mother; and he was always wandering up and down. I knew God was waiting to bless. I cast out the demon power, and heard long after that he had become quite well. Thus the blessed Holy Spirit takes us on from one place to another. So many things happen that I live in heaven on earth. Just the other day, at Coventry, God touched the people. Thus he takes us on, and on, and on.

Do not wait for inspiration if you are in need. The Holy Ghost is here, and you can have perfect deliverance as you sit in your seats. I was taken to three persons, one in the care of an attendant. As I entered the room there was a terrible din: quarrelling, such a noise it seemed as if all the powers of hell were stirred. I had to wait God's time. The Holy Ghost rose in me at the right time, and the three were delivered, and that night were singing praises to God. There had to be activity and testimony. Let it be known unto you that this man Christ is the same today.

Which man? God's Son, who has to have the glory, power, and dominion. "For he must reign, till he hath put all enemies under his feet" (1 Corinthians 15:25). When Jesus reigns in you, you know how to obey, how to work in conjunction with his will, his power, his light, his life. Having faith based upon knowledge, we know he has come—and in power. "Ye shall receive power, after that the Holy Ghost is come upon you" (Acts 1:8a).

We have experienced this power. Sometimes a fresh word comes to me. In the presence of a need, a revelation of the Spirit comes to my mind, "You shall be loosed." Loosed *now*. It looks like presumption, but God is with those who dare to stand upon his word. I remember, for instance, a woman who had not been able to smell anything for four years. I said, "You will smell now if you believe." This stirred another who had not smelled for twenty years. I said, "You will smell tonight." She went about smelling everything and was quite excited. Next day she gave her testimony.

At one place there was a man anointed for rupture. He came the next night, rose in the meeting, and said about me, "This man is an impostor; he is deceiving the people. He told me last night I was healed, but I am worse than ever today!" I spoke to the evil power that held the man and rebuked it, telling the man he was indeed healed. He was a stonemason. Next day he testified to lifting heavy weights, and that God had met him. It was the Word of God, not me, that he was against. "With his stripes we are healed" (Isaiah 53:5b).

"'What shall we do, that we might work the works of God?' Jesus answered... , 'This is the work of God, that ye believe on him whom he hath sent'" (John 6:28-29). Anything else? Yes.

He took our infirmities and healed all of our diseases. I myself am a marvel of healing. If I fail to glorify God, the very stones would cry out. Salvation is for all! Healing is for all! Baptism of the Holy Ghost is for all! Reckon yourselves dead indeed unto sin, but alive unto God. By his grace, get the victory every time. It is possible to live holy lives.

He breaks the power of cancelled sin,
He sets the prisoner free;
His blood can make the foulest clean,
His blood availed for me.

"'What shall we do, that we might work the works of God?' Jesus answered and said unto them, 'This is the work of God, that ye believe on him whom he hath sent.'"

THE MAN AND HIS MESSAGE

Originally titled "Faith Based on Knowledge" from *Confidence* (Sunderland, England), October-December 1919, pages 60-62. The editor of *Confidence* was Alexander A. Boddy, vicar of All Saints' Parish in Sunderland, where Smith Wigglesworth was baptized in the Holy Spirit in 1907.

During a 1928 tent meeting Wigglesworth conducted for the Anglican vicar W.H. Stuart-Fox, the overflowing crowd heard repeatedly the evangelist's emphasis on faith. Here is an excerpt from the vicar's report: "Mr. Wigglesworth was assisted by his daughter, Mrs. Salter, and her husband, who had carried out such a notable missionary work in the Congo. His deeply spiritual and profoundly moving addresses, and Mrs. Salter's vivacious, sparkling appeals, lit up by flashes of humour and homely illustrations, and so richly illustrated from Scriptures, largely helped to create the atmosphere in which Mr. Wigglesworth's call to 'faith as an act' might ring out its stirring note—challenging men and women to storm the very battlements of heaven and claim the full, rich, abundant life which God offers to all men in his Son Jesus Christ."[2]

FIVE

Building on the Word

"Now faith is the substance of things hoped for, the evidence of things not seen. For by it the elders obtained a good report. Through faith we understand that the worlds were framed by the word of God, so that things which are seen were not made of things which do appear" (Hebrews 11:1-3).

Beloved, if you are ever going to make any progress in the divine life, you must have a real foundation, and there is no foundation apart from faith. If you are standing on the Rock, no powers can move you, and there is no establishment for you outside of God's Word. Everything else is sand. If you build on anything else but the Word of God—on imaginations, sentimentality, feelings, or any special joy—it will mean nothing. You must have a foundation, and that foundation will have to be in the Word of God.

We are told that the Word of God shall stand forever, and not one jot or tittle of the Word shall fail. "Your Word is settled in heaven." In Psalm 138 we read, "Thou hast magnified thy word above all thy name" (vs 2). Also, if you turn to the first chapter of John's Gospel, verses 1-3, you will find a wonderful word: "In the beginning was the Word, and the Word was with God, and the Word was God. The same was in the beginning with God. All things were made by him; and without him was not any thing made that was made."

Here we have the foundation of all things, which is the Word. It is a substance. It is a power. It is a personality. It is a divine injunction to every soul that enters into this privilege, to be born of this Word, to be created of this Word, to have a knowledge of this Word.

What the Word means to us will be very important. For remember, it is a substance; it is the evidence of things not seen. It brings about that which is not there, and takes away that which is there. God, by his Word, made the world of things which did not appear, and we live in the world which he made, and which is inhabited by millions of people.

You say that this world is a substance. Jesus, the Word of God, made it of the things which do not appear. And there is nothing made that has not been made by that Word. When we come to the truth of what that Word means, we shall be able to know, and not only to *know* but also to *have*.

It helps me today to know that I am living in facts, I am moving in facts, I am in the knowledge of the principles of the Most High. God is a reality, and he is proving his mightiness in the midst of us. As we open ourselves to divine revelation and get rid of all things which are not of the Spirit, then we shall understand how mightily God can take us on in the Spirit and move the things which are and bring into prominence the things which are not.

Oh, the riches, the depths of the wisdom of the Most High! May he enlarge us this morning. God wants us to be so devoted to him that he can unveil himself. He rolls the clouds away; the mists depart at his presence. God is almighty in his movements. He has immensity of wisdom, unfolding the mysteries and the grandeur of his plan for the human race, that we may sink into insignificance, and that his mightiness may move upon us until we are the sons of God with power. Oh, this wonderful salvation! It is so beautiful.

THE WORD BECAME FLESH

What was the Word? The Word was Jesus. The Word became flesh and dwelt among us, and we saw and beheld the glory of God. Let me read to you from the Word of God: "That which was from the beginning, which we have heard, which we have seen with our eyes, which we have looked upon, and our hands have handled, of the Word of life; (For the life was manifested, and we have seen *it*, and bear witness, and show unto you that eternal life, which was with the Father, and was manifested unto us). That which we have seen and heard declare we unto you, that ye also may have fellowship with us: and truly our fellowship *is* with the Father, and with his Son, Jesus Christ" (1 John 1:1-3).

Oh, beloved, Jesus is the Word. He is the revelation sent forth from God. All fulness dwells in him. "Of his fulness have all we received, and grace for grace" (John 1:16). In weakness, strength; in poverty, wealth. Oh, brother and sister, this Word is a flame of fire! It may burn in your bones. It may move in every tissue of your life. Oh, the fact that I am begotten again and have become a son of God! Oh, how the whole creation groans for the manifestation of the sons of God! How we need the Word. The Word is life.

We read about Jesus Christ our Lord, that he was "declared *to be* the Son of God with power" (Romans 1:4a). Sons must have power. We must have power with God, power with our fellow creatures. We must have power over Satan, power over evil. You can never make evil pure. You cannot create impurity into purity. The carnal mind is not subject to the will of God, and cannot be. It must be destroyed.

It is most necessary that we should have the vision of God. The people have perished when there has been no vision. God wants us to have visions, revelations, and manifestations. You cannot have the Holy Ghost without manifestations and revelations. We must live in an anointing, a power, a transformation, and a divine attainment where God becomes wholly enthroned.

God cast Satan out of heaven because of his pride. Yes, beloved, but God could not have cast him out if Satan had been his equal in power. I tell you, beloved, we can never bind the strong man until we are in the place of binding. How was Satan cast out? By the Word of God's power. And, beloved, if we get to know and understand the principle of our inheritance by faith, we shall find out that Satan will always be cast out by the same power that cast him out in the beginning.

We need to eat and drink of this Word. We need to feed upon it in our hearts. We need that holy revelation that will take away the mist from our eyes and reveal Jesus. Don't forget that every day must be a day of advancement. If you have not made any advancement since yesterday, in a measure you are backsliding. There is only one way for you between Calvary and glory, between your conversion and heaven, and it is forward. We must catch the vision of the Master day by day. We must destroy everything that is not holy, for God wishes to seat us on high.

IN THE FURNACE OF AFFLICTION

The most trying time is the most helpful time. Beloved, if you read the Scriptures you will never find anything about an easy time, and if you are really reconstructed it will be in a hard time. It will not be in a singing meeting, but at a time when you think all things are dried up and that there is no hope for you. Then is the time that God makes the man or woman.

When we are tried by fire, God purges us, takes the dross away, and brings forth the pure gold. Only melted gold is useful. Only moistened clay receives the mold. Only softened wax receives the seal. Only broken, contrite hearts receive the mark as the Potter turns us on his wheel. We must have the stamp of our blessed Lord who was marred more than any other human being. He was truly the Son of God with power, with blessing, with life. He could take the weakest and make them strong.

God is here this morning in power, in blessing, and saying to you, "What is your request?" Oh, he is so precious! He never fails. Jesus is so gentle that he never breaks the bruised reed. He is so rich in his mighty benevolence that he makes the smoking flax to flame. Beloved, let me entreat you to pay any price. Never mind what it costs; it is worth all to have his smile, to have his presence.

Oh, you never need to be afraid of joining yourself to this Nazarene, for he is always a King. When Jesus was dying he was a King, and he said, "It is finished" (John 19:30b). Thank God, it is finished, and I know that because it is finished, everything is mine—things in heaven, things on earth, things under the earth. Jesus Christ is all power over all. He is in all. He is through all. Thank God, he is for all.

What are we going to do? Let the mantle fall from him onto you this day. Elijah said to Elisha, "If thou see me *when I am* taken from thee, it shall be so unto thee" (2 Kings 2:10). So Elisha kept his eye on Elijah. The mantle is to fall, my brothers and sisters, the mantle of power, the mantle of blessing. If your body is yielded sufficiently until it becomes perfectly the temple of the Holy Spirit, then the fulness will flow and his life shall be given to you as you need. May God help us all to believe this morning, not only for the rivers, but also for the mightiness of his unbounded ocean to flow through us.

THE MAN AND HIS MESSAGE

Originally titled "The Rock of Your Faith" from *Triumphs of Faith* (Oakland, California), October 1922, pages 223-26. Preached at Glad Tidings Temple in San Francisco. Originally titled "Faith," the sermon was revised and condensed by Carrie Judd Montgomery. A revival poster in a collection at the Assemblies of God Archives advertises Wigglesworth's later meetings at the temple, December 8-22, 1929, with two services a day and three on Sundays.

By 1925 Wigglesworth had preached around the world more than once. He was unknown when he went to New Zealand in 1922, but it is said that the pentecostal movement there began as a result of his meetings. The following report was given by an eyewitness, Harry Roberts: "The town hall in Wellington, seating three thousand, was engaged and the scenes that occurred nightly will long remain in our memories. The crowds were so great that the staff of the town hall were on duty, along with the police, to keep order. Not only were the seats occupied, but the passages were crowded, and over one thousand were addressed by Brother Lovelock and others outside. Many were saved outside, and a number came from all over the Dominion, and many remarkable cases of healing took place—in fact, all manner of sickness and disease was healed. In one meeting a call for the unsaved to stand and surrender to Christ and receive him as their personal Saviour resulted in about five hundred rising to their feet to signify their acceptance of him."[1]

SIX

Keep Your Eyes Fixed on Jesus

In 1 John 5:14-15 we read a very wonderful word: "And this is the confidence that we have in him, that, if we ask any thing according to his will, he heareth us: And if we know that he hear us, whatsoever we ask, we know that we have the petitions that we desired of him."

It is necessary that we find our bearings in this word. There is nothing that will give you such confidence as a life that is well pleasing to him. When Daniel's life pleased God, he could ask to be kept in the lions' den. But you cannot ask with confidence until there is a perfect union between you and God, as there was always perfect union between God and Jesus. The foundation is confidence in and fidelity to God.

Some people think that Jesus wept because of the love that he had for Lazarus, but that could not be. Jesus knew that these people who were around the grave, even Martha, had not come to the realization that whatever he would ask of the Father would be given to him. Their unbelief brought brokenness and sadness to the heart of Jesus; and he wept because of this. The moment you pray you find that the heavens are opened. If you have to *wait* for the heavens to be opened, something is wrong.

I tell you what makes us lose the confidence is disobedience to God and his laws. Jesus said it was because of those who stood around that he prayed; he himself knew that God heard him always. And because Jesus knew that his Father heard him always, he knew that the dead could come forth. At times there seems to be a stone wall in front of us. Everything seems as black as midnight, and there is nothing left but confidence in God. There is no feeling. What you must do is to have a fidelity and confidence to believe that he will not fail, indeed cannot fail.

We shall never get anywhere if we depend upon our feelings. There is something a thousand times better than feelings, and it is the naked Word of God. There is a divine revelation within you, that came in when you were born from above. To be born into the new kingdom is to be born into a new faith. Paul speaks of two classes of brethren, one of whom are obedient and the other disobedient. The obedient always obey God when he first speaks. It is the people of God whom he will use to make the world know that there is a God.

The just shall live by faith. You cannot talk about things which you have never experienced. It seems to me that God has a process of training us. You cannot take people into the depths of God unless you have been broken yourself. I have been broken and broken and broken. Praise God that he is near to those who are of a broken heart. You must have a brokenness to get into the depths of God.

There is a rest of faith, a faith that rests in confidence on God. God's promises never fail. "Faith cometh by hearing, and hearing by the word of God" (Romans 10:17). The Word of God can create a resistless faith, a faith that is never daunted, a faith that never gives up and never fails.

We fail to realize the largeness of our Father's measure, and we forget that he has a measure which cannot be exhausted. It pleases him when we ask for more. How much more? It is the "much more" that God shows me. I see that God has a plan of healing. It is on the line of a perfect confidence in him. The confidence comes not from our much speaking, but it comes because of our fellowship with him.

There is a wonderful fellowship with Jesus. The chief thing is to be sure that we take time for our communion with him. There is a communion with Jesus that is life, that is better than preaching. If God tells you definitely to do anything, do it, but be sure it is God who tells you.

GETTING OUT FROM UNDER THE BURDEN

I used to work with a man who had been a Baptist minister for twenty years. He was one of the sweetest souls I ever met. I used to walk by his side and listen to his instruction. God made the Word in his hand as a two-edged sword to me, and I used to say, "Yes, Lord." This man of God often pruned me with the sword of God, and it is just as sweet to me today as it was then.

If the sword ever comes to you, never straighten yourselves up against it, but let it pierce you. You must be yielded to the Word of God. The Word will work out love in our hearts, and when practical love is in our hearts there is no room to vaunt ourselves. We see ourselves as nothing when we become lost in this divine love. I praise God for the sword that pierces us and for a tender conscience.

Believers sometimes hurt each other by word or deed, but we can never let it rest until we make it right. Then we once again enjoy that sweetness of fellowship with Jesus. First, we need to be converted and to become as little children. We need to have the hard heart taken away, to have a heart that is broken and melted with the love of God.

This dear brother came to me one day and said, "The doctor says that this is the last day that my wife has to live." I said, "Oh, brother, why don't you believe God?"

He replied, "I have looked at you when you talked and have wept, and said, 'Father, if you could give me this confidence, I would be so happy.'" I said, "Could you trust God?" I felt that the Lord would heal his wife, so I asked another believer if he would accompany me in praying for this dying woman. I believed that if two of us would go and anoint her according to James 5:14-15, that she would be raised up. The man I asked to go with me said, "Oh, why do you come to me? I could not believe, although I believe the Lord would be sure to heal her if *you* would go." Then I sent for another man and asked him to go with me, and told him that whatever his impression was to be sure to pray through.[1] He prayed and agreed to go with me.

When we entered the house, I asked the man who had come with me to pray first. He cried in his desperation and prayed that this minister would be comforted after he was left with these motherless children, and that he might be strengthened to bear the sorrow! I could hardly wait until he had finished. My whole being was moved, and I thought, *What an awful thing to bring this man all this way to pray that kind of a prayer.*

What was the matter with him? He was looking at the dying woman instead of looking to God. You can never pray the prayer of faith if you look at the person who is needing it. There is only one place to look and that is to Jesus. The Lord wants to help us this afternoon to learn this truth and to keep our eyes on him.

When my prayer partner had finished, I said to my friend, "Now you pray." He took up the thread where the other man left off and went on with the same kind of petition. He got so down beneath the burden I thought he would never rise again, and I was glad when he got through.

I could not have borne it much longer. It all seemed out of order, the worst I had ever heard. My soul was stirred. I was anxious for God to get a chance to do something and to have his way. Rather than pray myself, I rushed to the bed, picked up the bottle of oil, and poured nearly the contents on the woman. I then saw Jesus just above the bed with the sweetest smile on his face. I said to her, "Woman, Jesus Christ makes you whole." And she was not only healed but was raised up that very hour.

Oh, beloved, may God help us this afternoon to get our eyes off the conditions and symptoms, no matter how bad they may be, and get them fastened upon him. Then we shall be able to pray the prayer of faith.

THE MAN AND HIS MESSAGE

From *Triumphs of Faith* (Oakland, California), August 1914, pages 175-77. This is one of the first sermons Wigglesworth preached in the United States, one which he gave at a Worldwide camp meeting in Cazadero, California. When he delivered this word in 1914, Wigglesworth was sorrowing over the death of his wife, Polly, the previous year. Little did he know that he would lose his son, George, the very next year.

SEVEN

A Living Hope

I want to call your attention to a very important subject that is found in 1 Peter 1:3. Here we read that God "hath begotten us again unto a living hope by the resurrection of Jesus Christ from the dead."

Now let us think about Paul's statements in 1 Corinthians 15 concerning the glorious fact of Christ, the first fruits. A farmer goes over his land eagerly scanning the budding ears of corn that show themselves above the soil. He knows that as the first beginnings are, so may the harvest be. And just in the measure as Jesus Christ is risen from the dead, so are we risen from the dead. As he is, so are we in this world. Christ is now getting the church ready for translation.

Here we read in 1 Peter 1:3, "We are begotten again into a living hope by the resurrection of Jesus Christ from the dead." Oh, to be changed—a living fact in the body, just as in the flesh Jesus triumphed by the Spirit. Oh, to be like him! What a living hope it is! Paul and Peter were together very little, but both were inspired to bring before the church this wonderful truth of the living being changed. If Christ rose not, we are yet in our sins; our faith is in vain, it has no foundation. But Christ *has* risen and become the first fruits, and we have now the glorious hope that *we* shall be so changed.

We who were not a people are now the people of God: born out of due time, out of the mire, to be among princes. Beloved, God wants us to see how precious this is. It will drive away the dullness of life; it is here set above all other things. Jesus gave all for this treasure. He purchased the field because of the pearl, the pearl of great price—the substratum of humanity. Jesus purchased it, and we are that pearl of great price for all time. Our inheritance is in heaven, and in 1 Thessalonians 4:18 we are told to "comfort one another with these words."

AN INHERITANCE INCORRUPTIBLE

What can you have better in the world than the hope that in a little while this glorious change will come? It seems such a short time since I was a boy; in a little while I shall be changed by his grace and be more than a conqueror in "an inheritance incorruptible, and undefiled, and that fadeth not away" (1 Peter 1:4). The inheritance is in you, something that is done for you, accomplished by God for you. A work of God wrought out for us by himself, an inheritance incorruptible.

When my daughter was in Africa, she often wrote of things corroding. We have a corruptible nature, but, as the natural decays, the spiritual nature is at work. As the corruptible is doing its work, we are changing. When will it be seen? When Jesus comes. Most beautiful of all, we shall be like him. What is the process? Grace! What can work it out? Love! Love! Love! It cannot be rendered in human phrases. God so loved that he gave Jesus.

There is something very wonderful about being undefiled: there in the presence of my King to be undefiled, never to change, only to become more beautiful. Unless we know something about grace and the omnipotence of God's love, we should never be able to grasp it. Love is fathomless as the sea, grace flowing for you and for me. He has prepared a place for us, a place which will fit in beautifully, with no fear of anyone else taking it. It is reserved.

When I went to a certain meeting I had a seat reserved and numbered. I could walk in any time. What is there in the reserving? Having a place where we can see God, the very seat we would have chosen. He knows just what we want! There will be no brokenness or upset or wish to have come sooner. He has made us for that very moment, the beginning of all joys. He loved me so; no sadness throughout all eternity.

Will we be there? Is it possible for us to miss it? We are "kept by the power of God through faith unto salvation ready to be revealed in the last time" (1 Peter 1:5). What is peculiar about it? The fulness of perfection, the ideal of love, the beatitudes worked into us. The poor in spirit, the mourners, the meek, the hungry and thirsty, the merciful, the pure—all ready to be revealed at the appearing of Jesus Christ.

You could not remain there but for the purifying, the perfecting, the establishing—God working out his perfect will when ready! Refined enough, you will go. But there is something to be done yet to establish you, to make you purer. A great price has been paid. The trial of your faith is more precious than gold that perishes. And men are losing their heads for gold all the time.

And we must give all, yield all, as our great refiner puts us again and again into the melting pot. What for? To lose the dross, that the pure gold of his presence be clearly seen and his glorious image reflected—from glory to glory even by the Spirit of the Lord. We must be steadfast, immovable, until all his purposes are accomplished.

Praising God along these lines while you're sitting in a meeting is altogether different from the time when you are faced with a hard course. There must be no perishing though we are tried by fire. What will be revealed at the appearing of Jesus? Faith!

Faith! The establishing of your heart by the grace of the Spirit, not to crush, but to refine; not to destroy, but to enlarge you.

FAITH TRIED BY FIRE

Oh, beloved, to make you know the enemy as a defeated foe, and Jesus not only conquering but displaying the spoils of conquest! The pure in heart shall see God. If your eye be single, your whole body shall be full of light.

What brings us to this place? Loyalty to the Word by the power of the blood. You know your inheritance within you is more powerful than all that is without. How many have gone to the stake and perished through fiery persecution? Did they desire it? Faith tried by fire had power to withstand all ridicule, all slander. The faith of the Son of God who "for the joy that was set before him endured the cross" (Hebrews 12:2b). Oh, the joy of pleasing him. No trial, no darkness, nothing too hard for us.

If only I may see the image of my Lord in it again and again. He removes the skimmings until in the melting pot his face is seen. When my heart reflects him, it is pure. Who is looking into our hearts? Who is the refiner? My Lord. He will remove only that which will hinder. Oh, I know the love of God is working out in my heart a great purpose of reality.

I remember going to the Crystal Palace when General Booth reviewed the representatives of the Salvation Army from all nations. It was a grand sight as company after company with all their peculiar characteristics passed a certain place where he could view them. It was a wonderful scene. Likewise, we are going to be presented to God. The trials are getting us ready for the procession and the presentation. We are to be a joy to look at, to be to his praise and glory. No one will be there but those tried by fire.

Is it worth it? Yes, a thousand times, yes! Oh, the ecstasy of exalted pleasure! God thus reveals himself to our hearts. First Peter 1:22 speaks of unfeigned faith and unfeigned love. What it means to have unfeigned faith! When ill-used, put to shame, or whatever the process, it never alters, only to be more refined, more like unto him. Unfeigned love full of appreciation for those who do not see eye to eye with us. "Father, forgive them" (Luke 23:34a). Remember Stephen: "Lay not this sin to their charge" (Acts 7:60).

Unfeigned love is the greatest thing God can bestow on our hearts. The twenty-third verse tells us we are saved by a power incorruptible—a process always refining, a grace always enlarging, a glory always increasing. Thus we are made neither barren nor unfruitful, in the knowledge of our Lord Jesus Christ.

The spirits of just men made perfect will be garnered in the treasury of the Most High. Purified as sons. To go out no more. To be as he is—holy, blameless. And it will be through all eternity to gaze upon him with pure, unfeigned love. God glorified in our midst, as the whole company of heaven cries out: "Holy, holy, holy, Lord God almighty" (Revelation 4:8b). "And this is the word which by the gospel is preached unto thee" (1 Peter 1:25b). How can we be sad, or hang our heads, or be distressed? Oh, if we only knew how rich we are! Blessed be the name of the Lord.

THE MAN AND HIS MESSAGE

Originally titled "Our Living Hope" from *Confidence* (Sunderland, England), May-June 1917, pages 37-39. Preached that March at Wigglesworth's Bowland Street Mission in Bradford.

Following World War I, Wigglesworth resumed his international travels. In April 1921 he went to Stockholm, Sweden, under the auspices of Lewi Pethrus, a former Baptist minister who would become one of the pentecostal leaders in the world. Stockholm authorities arrested Wigglesworth for laying hands on the sick during his public prayer lines. Wigglesworth was

continued on page 78

released, but Pethrus was interrogated concerning the possibility that Wigglesworth was using hypnosis. They also questioned the use of anointing handkerchiefs for the sick who were unable to attend the meetings. After consultation with the medical board, the investigating authorities decided to drop the charges. However, Wigglesworth's application for an extension of his visa was denied, and he was told that he could not lay hands on the sick in a mass meeting conducted in a public park on Whitmonday (the day after Pentecost Sunday).

"I knew that God was not limited to my laying hands on the people," Wigglesworth said. "When the presence of the Lord is there to heal it does not require the laying on of hands. Faith is the great operating factor. When we believe God, all things are easy." Wigglesworth originated a new procedure as a result of the meeting in Stockholm: he told the estimated twenty thousand people that if they were sick, they were to lay hands on themselves and he would pray a prayer of faith. This procedure proved useful in crowded meetings around the world.[1]

PART TWO:

Putting Faith
into Action

EIGHT

The Power of Possibility

I t is a great joy to be with the saints of God, especially those who have come into "like precious faith" to believe that God is almighty. Beloved, we may be in a very low ebb of the tide, but it is good to be in a place where the tide can rise.

I pray that the Holy Ghost shall so have his right of way that there will not be one person in this tent who shall not be moved upon by the Spirit of God. Everything depends upon our being filled with the Holy Ghost. And there is nothing you can come short of if the Holy Ghost is the prime mover in your thoughts and life, for he has a plan greater than ours. And if he can only get us in readiness for his plan to be worked out, it will be wonderful.

Let us focus on Hebrews 11:1-10 for this message. This is a very remarkable word to us! Faith. Everything depends upon our believing God. If we are saved, it is only because God's Word says so. We cannot rest upon our feelings. We cannot do anything without a living faith. It is surely God himself who comes to us in the person of his beloved Son and so strengthens us that we realize that our bodies are surrounded by the power of God lifting us into his almighty power. All things are possible to us in God.

The purpose of God for us is that we might be in the earth for the manifestation of his glory, that every time satanic power is confronted, God might be able to ask of us as he did of Job, "What do you think about him?" God wants us to so manifest his divine plan in the earth that Satan shall have to hear God. The joy of the Lord can be so overflowing in us and we shall be so filled with God that we shall be able to rebuke the power of the devil.

EVERYTHING THAT IS NOT OF FAITH IS SIN

God has reminded me in the night watches that everything that is not of faith is sin. I have seen this in the Word so many times. God wants to bring us into harmony with his will so that we will line up with the Word of God, to believe it all. If there is something within us that is not purely sanctified, God wants it to be changed by the power of the Word. Many people are putting their human wisdom in the place of God, and God is not able to give the best because the human is so often confronting God. God is not able to get the best through us until the human is dissolved.

"Faith is the substance of things hoped for" (Hebrews 11:1). I want to speak about "substance." It is a remarkable word. "I want things that are tangible," people say to me. "I want something to appeal to my human reasoning." Beloved, everything that you cannot see is eternal. Everything that you can see is natural and fades away. Everything you see in this tent will fade away and will be consumed, but that which you cannot see, which is more real than you, is the substance of all things. This faith is God in the human soul, mightier than you by a million times.

Beloved, we have to go out and be faced with evil powers.

Even your own heart, if it is not entirely immersed in the Spirit, will deceive you. So I am praying that there shall not be a vestige of your human nature that shall not be clothed by the power of the Spirit. I pray that the Spirit of the living God may be so imparted to your heart that nothing shall in any way be able to move you after this meeting. "Faith is the substance of things hoped for, the evidence of things not seen."

God has mightily blessed me because I know what Peter meant in his first epistle: "Being born again, not of corruptible seed, but of incorruptible, by the word of God, which liveth and abideth for ever" (1 Peter 1:23). We read in John 1:1, "In the beginning was the Word, and the Word was with God, and the Word was God." Then in verse fourteen we read that "the Word was made flesh, and dwelt among us, (and we beheld his glory, the glory as of the only begotten of the Father,) full of grace and truth." Jesus Christ is in the midst of us manifested. His disciples went out and confirmed that they had seen and touched him, the Word of life.

If you turn to 2 Peter 1:4, you will find that we have received his divine nature, which is infinite power, infinite knowledge, infinite pleasure, infinite revelation. But people are missing it because they have failed to apply it. God is forming a people who will be a "first fruits."

By simple faith you entered in and claimed your rights and became Christians, being born again because you believed. But there is something different in *knowing* God, in having fellowship with him. There are heights and depths in this wonderful blessing in the knowledge of him. We experience human weakness, helplessness, impossibility. The Holy Ghost wants everybody to see the unveiling of Jesus. The unveiling of Jesus is to take away ourselves and to place himself in us, to take away all our human weakness and put within us that wonderful Word of eternal power, of eternal life, which makes us believe that all things are possible.

FAITH IS THE SUBSTANCE OF THINGS HOPED FOR

A man who was a dealer in racehorses traveled with me from Montreal to Vancouver and then by ship to New Zealand. It seemed he could not leave me. He was frivolous and talked about races and other things of the world, but he could not keep up his end of the conversation. I did not struggle to keep up my end because mine is a living power. No person who has Jesus as the inward power of his body needs to tremble when Satan comes around. All he or she has to do is to stand still and see the salvation of the Lord.

Reaching a certain island of the Fiji group, we all went ashore and God gave me wonderful liberty in preaching. The man came back afterwards, but he did not go to his racing and card-playing chums. He came stealing back to the ship and with tears in his eyes, he said to me, "I am dying. I have been bitten by a snake." Indeed, his skin had turned to a dark green and his leg was swollen. "Can you help me?" he cried.

If we only knew the power of God! If we are in a place of substance, of reality, of ideal purpose. It is not human; we are dealing with the Almighty. I have a present God. I have a living faith. And the living faith is the Word, and the Word is life, and the Word is equipment, and the Lord is just the same "yesterday, and today, and for ever" (Hebrews 13:8).

Placing my hand upon the serpent bite, I said, "In the name of Jesus, come out!" The man looked at me and the tears came. The swelling went down before his eyes and he was perfect in a moment.

"Faith is the substance of things hoped for, the evidence of things not seen." Faith is that which came into me when I believed. I was born of the incorruptible Word by the living virtue, life, and personality of God. I was instantly changed from nature to grace. I became a servant of God and I became an enemy of unrighteousness.

The Holy Ghost wants us to clearly understand that we are a

million times bigger than we know. No Christian in this place has any conception of what he or she is. My heart is so big that I want to look into your faces and tell you that if you only knew what you had, your bodies would scarcely be able to contain it. Oh, that God shall so bring us into divine attractiveness by his almightiness that the whole of our bodies shall wake up to resurrection force, to the divine, inward flow of eternal power coursing through the human frame.

CLOTHED WITH POWER FROM ON HIGH

Let us read Ephesians 4:7-8, 11-13: "But unto every one of us is given grace according to the measure of the gift of Christ. Wherefore he saith, When he ascended up on high, he led captivity captive, and gave gifts unto men.... And he gave some, apostles; and some, prophets; and some, evangelists; and some, pastors and teachers; For the perfecting of the saints, for the work of the ministry, for the edifying of the body of Christ: Till we all come in the unity of the faith, and of the knowledge of the Son of God, unto a perfect man, unto the measure of the stature of the fulness of Christ."

God took you into his pavilion and began to clothe you and give you the gifts of the Spirit, that in ministering by the power of God you should bring all the church into the perfect possession of the fulness of Christ. Oh, the wonder of it! Oh, the adaptability of his equipment!

Tongues with interpretation: *"God has designed it. In the pavilion of his splendor, with the majesty of his glory he comes, and touching human weakness, beautifies it in the spirit of holiness till the effectiveness of this wonderful sonship is made manifest in us, till we all become the embodiment of the fulness of Christ."*

I believe God wants you to have something this morning that could never happen unless you cease to be for yourself. God wants you to be for him, to be for everybody. But, oh, to have the touch of God! Beloved, the Holy Ghost is the Comforter. The Holy Ghost came not to speak of himself, but he came to unveil him who said, "Take my yoke upon you, and learn of me; for I am meek and lowly in heart: and ye shall find rest unto your souls" (Matthew 11:29).

The Holy Ghost came to thrill you with resurrection power, that you should be anointed with fresh oil running over in the splendor of his almightiness. Then right through you shall come forth a river of divine unction that shall sustain you in the most bitter place, and quicken the dead formality, and say to the weak, "Be strong," and to those who suffer loss, "The Lord of hosts is here to comfort you." God would have us to be like the rising of the sun, filled with the rays of heaven, all the time beaming forth the gladness of the Spirit of the Almighty. Possibility is the greatest thing of your life.

When I came into the tent yesterday afternoon, no one else could understand my feelings. Was it emotion? No, it was an inward inspiration to find hearts that God had touched, those who had met me with such love. It was almost more than I could bear. I have to thank God for it and take courage that he has been with me in the past, and he will be with me in the future.

Brothers and sisters, I am satisfied that love is the essential. Love is of God; nay, love *is* God. Love is the Trinity working in the human heart to break it, that it may be filled with God's fulness.

When you hear me tell stories of people who were healed and delivered, you might ask, "Can he do it for me?" Yes, if you believe. Beloved, faith is the victory. Here I am, so thankful this morning. Thirty years ago this body you see was sick and helpless and dying. God, in an instant, healed me. I am now sixty-five years within a day or two and so free and healthy. Oh, it is wonderful! There are people in this place who ought to be healed in a moment, people who ought to receive the Holy Ghost in a moment.

The power of possibility is within the reach of every man and woman here. The Holy Ghost is a rising tide. Every one of us can be filled to overflowing. God is here with his divine purpose to change our weakness into mighty strength and faith. The Word of God! Oh, brother, sister, have you got it? It is marrow to your bones. It is unction. It is resurrection from every weakness. It is life from the dead.

If there is anything I want to shake you loose from, it is having a word of faith without the power of it. What are we here for? Surely we are not to hear only; we are to obey. Obedience is better than sacrifice. God the Holy Ghost would give us such a revelation of Christ that we would go away as people who had seen the King. We would go away with our faces lit up with the brilliancy of heaven.

How many in this place are willing to believe? If you would like God to know you are sincere and will do whatever his Spirit tells you, rise up and walk to the front and cry to God until you have all you want. Let God have his way. Touch God this morning. Faith is the victory.

THE MAN AND HIS MESSAGE

Originally titled "Faith Is the Victory" from *Triumphs of Faith* (Oakland, California), June 1924, pages 126-31. Preached at the Pentecostal Camp Meeting, Berkeley, California, on June 1, this sermon was abridged by Carrie Judd Montgomery and printed by Glad Tidings Temple in San Francisco.

You will notice in this and other chapters the heading, "tongues with interpretation." Frequently during the course of Wigglesworth's sermons, he would suddenly speak in tongues and then give the interpretation (1 Corinthians 12:14). Some editors for various reasons have chosen to delete these charismatic manifestations when publishing Wigglesworth's sermons. I have included them when possible.

NINE

Making a Pest
of Yourself

What would happen to us and to the needy world if we should get to the place where we really believed God? May God give us the desire to get to this place. Faith is a tremendous power, an inward mover. I am convinced that we have not yet seen all that God has for us, but if we shall only move on in faith, we shall see the greater works.

When I was a little boy I remember asking my father for a pennyworth of something or other. He did not give it to me, so I sat down by his side and every now and again I would just quietly say, "Father!" He would appear to take no notice of me, but now and again I would touch him ever so gently and say, "Father!"

My mother said to him, "Why don't you answer the child?" My father replied, "I have done so, but he won't accept my answer." Still I sat there, and occasionally I would touch him and say, ever so quietly, "Father!" If he went out into the garden I followed him, and occasionally I would touch his sleeve and say, "Father! Father!!" Do you think I ever went away without the accomplishment of my desire? No, not once.

We need the same importunity as we go to God. We have the blessed assurance that if we ask anything according to his will he hears us. And if we know that God hears us, whatsoever we ask, we know that we have the petitions we desire of him.

Do you go to God for heart purity? It is his will that you should receive, and if you ask in faith you can know that you have the petition that you desire of him. Do you desire that Christ should dwell in your heart by faith? That is in accordance with his will. Ask and you shall receive. Do you desire that the might of God's Spirit shall accompany your ministry? That is according to the will of God.

Continue in the presence of your heavenly Father, quietly reminding him that this is what you desire, and he will not fail to give you an exceeding abundance, above all you ask or think. He will fill you with rivers—the blessed rivers of the Spirit—and flowing from the midst of you, they will be blessings to all around.

FAITH IS LIKE DYNAMITE

In the introduction to his second epistle, Peter addresses "[those who] have obtained like precious faith with us" (2 Peter 1:1). It is written, "They that trust in the Lord *shall be* as mount Zion, *which* cannot be removed" (Psalm 125:1). Have you this faith of divine origin springing up in your heart? It will make you steadfast and unmovable. This faith, this confidence, this trust in God, will have a transforming power, changing and transforming spirit, soul, and body, sanctifying the entire being.

"Faith *cometh* by hearing, and hearing by the Word of God" (Romans 10:17). It is God coming in by his Word and laying the solid foundation. Faith is like dynamite which breaks up the old life and nature by the power of God, and brings the almighty power of God into that life. This substance will diffuse through the whole being, bringing everything else into insignificance.

The Word of God is formed within the temple. Jeremiah spoke of the Word as a fire within. It is a power stronger than granite that is able to resist the mightiest pressure the devil can bring against it. Faith counts on God's coming forth to confound the enemy. Faith counts on the display of God's might when it is needful for him to come forth in power.

In these eventful days we must not be content with a mere theory of faith, but must have this almighty and precious faith within us so that we may move from the ordinary into the extraordinary. We must expect God to come forth in power through us for the deliverance of others. Peter spoke of it as "like precious faith" (2 Peter 1:1). It is a like kind to that which Abraham had—the very faith of God. When Peter said to the lame man, "Such as I have give I thee: In the name of Jesus Christ of Nazareth rise up and walk" (Acts 3:6), there was a manifestation of the same faith that Abraham had. It is this kind of precious faith that God wants us to have.

In the former days the prophets received the Holy Spirit in a certain measure, but the Holy Spirit was given to the Lord Jesus Christ without measure. Did not he give the Holy Spirit on the day of Pentecost in this same measure? That is his thought for you and me. Since I received the mighty baptism in the Holy Spirit, God has flooded my life with his power. From time to time there have been wonderful happenings—to him be all the glory. Faith in God will bring the operation of the Spirit and we will have the divine power flooding the human vessel and flowing out in blessing to others.

Faith is made in hard places when we are at wit's end, when there seems no way out of our adversity. David said at one time, "The sorrows of death compassed me, and the floods of ungodly men made me afraid. The sorrows of hell compassed me about" (Psalm 18:4-5). He testifies, "In my distress I called upon the Lord, and cried unto my God: he heard my voice out of his temple.... He bowed the heavens... and came down" (vs 6, 9).

Faith cries to God in the place of testing. It is in these places that God enlarges us and brings us forth into a large place, to prove himself the God of deliverances, the one who is indeed our help.

I remember in the year 1920 after a most distressing voyage, I went straight to a meeting from the ship on which I had been traveling. As I entered the building a man fell down across the doorway in a fit. The Spirit of the Lord was upon me and I commanded the demon to leave. Some years later I visited this same assembly, and I ventured to ask if anyone remembered the incident. That same man stood, and I told him to come to the platform. He told me that on that day he had been delivered by the name of Jesus and had not had a fit since.

We read in Acts 10:38 that "God anointed Jesus of Nazareth with the Holy Ghost and with power. [He] went about doing good, and healing all that were oppressed of the devil; for God was with him." God wants us to have this same anointing and this same power through the indwelling Christ and through a living faith. It was the Lord himself who told us before he went away, "These signs shall follow them that believe; In my name shall they cast out devils... they shall lay hands on the sick, and they shall recover" (Mark 16:17-18).

God is waiting to manifest his divine power through believers. I remember a man coming to me suffering with cancer who said he had been in pain for twelve years. The power of the Lord was present to heal, and that night he came back to the meeting with all his sores dried up.

In this Second Epistle of Peter we further read, "According as his divine power hath given unto us all things that *pertain* unto life and godliness, through the knowledge of him that hath called us to glory and virtue: Whereby are given unto us exceeding great and precious promises that by these ye might be partakers of the divine nature" (2 Peter 1:3-4a). Believe the record. His divine power has provided this life and godliness and virtue.

Believe for the virtue of the Lord to be so manifested through your body, that as people touch you they are healed. Believe for the current to go through you to others.

It is amazing what can happen when some necessity arises, when there is no time to pray, only to act. It is in such times of necessity that the Holy Ghost comes forth to act. We must so live in God that the Spirit of God can operate through us. I remember being in one place where there were six thousand people outside the building where we were preaching. Many of them were in chairs, waiting for hands to be laid on them and the prayer of faith to be offered. Oh, for the virtue that flowed from Christ to touch the needy everywhere!

HEAR GOD'S WORD AND KEEP IT

A woman said to Christ one time, "Blessed is the womb that bare thee, and the paps which thou hast sucked" (Luke 11:27b). But Jesus answered, "Yea, rather, blessed *are* they that hear the word of God and keep it" (vs 28). It is through the hearing of the Word of God that faith comes, and faith brings the omnipotence of God to helpless souls and brings the virtue of Christ to the sick and the needy.

Do you remember how they asked the Lord, "'What shall we do, that we might work the works of God?' Jesus answered and said unto them, 'This is the work of God, that ye believe on him whom he hath sent'" (John 6:28-29). He further said, "The works that I do shall [you] do also; and greater *works* than these shall [you] do; because I go unto my Father" (John 14:12). There is nothing impossible to faith.

When I was in Orebro [Sweden] twelve years ago, I ministered to a blind girl who was twelve years old. When I last went to Orebro they told me that she had perfect sight from that day. The Lord himself challenges us to believe him when he says, "Have faith in God." "Verily I say unto you, that whosoever shall say unto this mountain, 'Be thou removed, and be thou cast into the sea'; and shall not doubt in his heart, but shall believe that those things which he saith shall come to pass; he shall have whatsoever he saith" (Mark 11:23).

Did you get that? "He shall have whatsoever he says." When you speak in faith, your desire is an accomplished thing. Our Lord added in verse twenty-four, "Therefore I say unto you, What things soever you desire, when ye pray, believe that ye receive *them,* and ye shall have *them.*" Have you received this "like precious faith"? If so, deal bountifully with the oppressed. God has called us to loose the bonds of wickedness, undo the heavy burden, let the oppressed go free, and break the yokes that the devil has put upon them. Pray in faith.

Remember: those who ask receive. Ask and it shall be given you. Live for God. Keep yourself clean and holy. Live under the unction of the Holy Spirit. Let the mind of Christ be yours so that you live in God's desires and plans. Glorify him in the establishment of his blessing upon the people, and in seeing God's glory manifested in our midst. Amen.

THE MAN AND HIS MESSAGE

Originally titled "Like Precious Faith" from the *Pentecostal Evangel* (Springfield, Missouri), May 13, 1933, pages 2-3.

Well-known for his bold faith, Wigglesworth would often command cripples and others to walk or even run after he had prayed for them. At times his well-meaning actions turned humorous. Leland Keys, a former pastor of Glad Tidings Temple in San Francisco, told of a woman who came to Wigglesworth on crutches. After prayer, Wigglesworth took the crutches, turned her around, and ordered her to walk up the aisle to demonstrate her healing. "To get her started he placed both hands on her back and gave her a solid push. Apparently the dear sister felt she did not need that kind of help. She turned around and took a full swing at Brother Wigglesworth, just missing his jaw by inches."[1]

TEN

Faith That Delivers

O ur text is from the great faith chapter of Hebrews: "By faith Enoch was translated that he should not see death; and was not found, because God had translated him: for before his translation he had this testimony, that he pleased God" (Hebrews 11:5).

Without faith it is impossible to please God. The person who comes to God must believe that God is. I want to encourage you to believe also that he is able to work out his plan in your life. He will work mightily through you, if you believe. Great possibilities are within your reach if you dare to believe.

Evil spirits can have no more control over me, if I believe that God is, that he is living and active; and I do. I know I am free from all the powers of darkness, free from all the powers of evil, and it is a wonderful thing to be free. Christ said, "Ye shall know the truth, and the truth shall make you free" (John 8:32). Because you are free, you can step into the liberty of freed men and women and claim the possessions of God.

This is the dispensation of the Holy Ghost. It is thirty-three years since God filled me with the Holy Ghost. The fire burned in my bosom then and it is still burning, producing more activity for God than it did in 1907. The Holy Spirit is not played out.

95

God is waiting for people who dare to believe, and when you believe, all things are possible.

Only believe, only believe,
All things are possible, only believe.
Only believe, only believe,
All things are possible, only believe.

God wants to sweep away all unbelief from your heart, for you to dare to believe his Word. It is the Word of the Spirit. If you allow anything to come in between you and the Word, it will poison your whole system, and you will have no hope. One bit of unbelief against that Word is poison. It is like the devil putting a spear into you. The Word of life is the breath of heaven, the quickening power by which your very life is changed, and you begin to bear the image of the heavenly.

OVERCOMING FAITH

A young man in South Africa who was dying of consumption read my book *Ever-Increasing Faith*. He was saved and then God healed him. This young man grew so in the knowledge of God that he became a pastor. When I arrived in South Africa five years ago, he came up to me like a son to a father and said, "If you like, I will go with you all over South Africa."

He bought the best car for the job. If you go to South Africa, you must have a car to go through the plowed fields, one that will jump the hedges, jump into the river, and jump out again. That young man drove us five thousand miles through all the territories, right along the Zulus, and God took us through everything. Talk about life. Why, this is overcoming life!

When I arrived in Capetown, I saw a man whose deathly face was filled with the very devil's manifestation of cancer. I said to the people, "There is a man in this place suffering with a tremendous thing. He does not know I am talking about him at all. You can have the choice. If you desire me to deliver that man, so that he can enjoy the meeting, I will go down in the name of the Lord and deliver him, or else I will preach."

They said, "Come down." So I went down and the people saw what God can do, saw that man shouting, raving, for he was like a man who was intoxicated. He was shouting, "I am free! I have been bound." It was a wonderful thing to see that man changed.

Another man came in great need that night. After laying out forty-five hundred dollars for his wife to have operation after operation, year by year, he brought her helpless to the meeting. I went to her and said, "Look here, this is the greatest opportunity of your life. I will give an altar call tonight. There will be fifty people who come up, and when you see them loosed, you will believe, and you will be loosed like them, and then we shall have a testimony from you."

The fifty came and I laid my hands upon them in the name of the Lord. I said, "Testify," and they testified. This woman saw their faces, and when all these people were through I turned to her and asked, "Do you believe?" She said, "I cannot help but believe." There is something in the manifestation of faith. I laid hands upon her in the name of Jesus and the power of God went right through her. I said, "In the name of Jesus, arise and walk."

An impossibility? If you do not venture, you remain ordinary as long as you live. If you dare the impossible, then God will abundantly do far above all you ask or think. As if a cannon had blown her up, this woman rose from her seat. I thought her husband would go mad with joy and excitement because he saw his wife mightily moved by the power of God and made free. She was in the first meeting afterwards to glorify God.

The divine plan is so much greater than all human thought. When we are willing to yield to his sovereign will, when we have no reserve, how wonderful God is, always willing to open the door till our whole life is filled with the fragrance of heaven.

Jesus is the substance and fulness of the divine nature, and he dwells in our hearts. Oh, this wonderful, fascinating Jesus! What a wonderful Jesus we have! Something about him kindles fire in the darkest place. Something about our Lord makes all darkness light. When we have him we have more than we can speak about or think about. God's Son can set the world ablaze and bring heaven right into the place where we live. Dare to believe God, and nothing shall be impossible to you.

THE MAN AND HIS MESSAGE

From the *Pentecostal Evangel* (Springfield, Missouri), June 21, 1941, page 4. From evidence in the text, this sermon was apparently preached in 1940.

If Wigglesworth knew his hearers needed encouragement to believe, or if others questioned his theology, this man known as the "Apostle of Faith" had a stock answer: "God says it; I believe it; and that settles it."

His faith went forth in other ways as well. It has been said that Wigglesworth gave away more money than he kept. His book royalties supported missions in the Congo (now Zaire). And no doubt profits from his only known commercial venture—the "Wigglesworth Leak-Proof Anointing Bottle"—also went back into some type of ministry. Believers who prayed for the sick could order the bottle for one dollar from the Glad Tidings Book Room, San Francisco (the "sole agents in this country" according to the 1920s advertisement).[1]

ELEVEN

Become an Overcomer

I n the first chapter of Mark we read of John the Baptist, a man who was filled with the Holy Spirit from his mother's womb. Because of this mighty infilling there was a mighty message on his lips. The prophet Isaiah had foretold of John that he would be the voice of one crying in the wilderness. He was to lift up his voice with strength and cry to the cities of Judah, "Behold your God!" (Isaiah 40:9b).

And so we find John as he pointed to Jesus, crying out, "Behold the Lamb of God" (John 1:36b), proclaiming him to be the one of whom Abraham prophesied when he said to his son, Isaac, "God will provide himself a lamb" (Genesis 22:8a)—the Lamb of God and God the Lamb.

John was so filled with the Spirit of God that the cry he raised moved all Israel. This shows that when God gets hold of people and fills them with the Spirit, they can have a cry, a message, a proclamation of the gospel that will move others. Those who do not have the Spirit of the Lord may cry for fifty years and see nobody take notice of them. The one who is filled with the

Spirit of God needs to cry out but once and people will feel the effect of it.

This should teach us that there is a necessity for every one of us to be filled with the Spirit of God. It is not sufficient just to have a touch or to have a desire. There is only one thing that will meet the needs of people today, and that is to be immersed in the life of God—God taking you and filling you with his Spirit, until you live right in God and God lives in you—so that whether you eat or drink or whatever you do, it shall be all for the glory of God.

In that place you will find that all your strength and all your mind and all your soul are filled with zeal, not only for worship, but to proclaim the gospel message, a proclamation that is accompanied by the power of God—which must defeat satanic power, discomfit the world, and redound to the glory of God.

THE MASTER MODEL

The reason the world today is not seeing Jesus is because believers are not filled with the Spirit of Christ. They are satisfied with going to church, occasionally reading the Bible, and sometimes praying. Beloved, if God lays hold of you by the Spirit, you will find that there is an end to everything of the old life. All the old things will have passed away, and all things will have become new. All things are of God.

You will find that as you are wholly yielded to God, your whole being will be transformed by the divine indwelling. He will take you in hand so that you may become a vessel unto honor. Our lives are not to be for ourselves. If we live for self, we shall die. If we seek to save our lives, we shall lose them; but if we lose our lives, we shall save them. If we through the Spirit mortify the deeds of the body, we shall live: live a life of freedom and joy and blessing and service, a life that will bring blessing to others.

God would have us see that we must be filled with the Spirit, every day live in the Spirit and walk in the Spirit, and be continually renewed in the Spirit. Study the life of Jesus. It was quite a natural thing for him, after he had served a whole day among the multitude, to want to go to his Father to pray all night.

Why? Jesus wanted a renewing of divine strength and power. He wanted fellowship with his Father. His Father would speak to him the word that he was to bring to others, and would empower him afresh for new ministry. Jesus would come from those hours of sweet communion and fellowship with his Father, clothed with his holy presence and Spirit, and anointed with the Holy Spirit and power. Then he would go about doing good and healing all who were oppressed of the enemy.

When Jesus met sickness it had to leave. He came from that holy time of communion with power to meet the needs of the people, whatever they were. It is an awful thing for me to see people who profess to be Christians lifeless and powerless. The place of holy communion is open to us all. There is a place where we can be daily refreshed and renewed and reempowered.

In the fourth chapter of Hebrews we are told, "There remaineth therefore a rest to the people of God. For he that is entered into his rest, he also hath ceased from his own works" (vs 9-10). Oh, what a blessed rest that is, to cease from your own works, to come to the place where God is now enthroned in your life, working in you day by day to will and to do his good pleasure, working in you an entirely new order of things.

God wants to bring you forth as a flame of fire, with a message from God, with a truth that shall defeat the powers of Satan, with an unlimited supply for every needy soul. Just as John moved the whole of Israel with a mighty cry, you too by the power of the Holy Ghost can move the people so that they repent and cry, "What shall we do?"

This is what Jesus meant when he said to Nicodemus, "Except a man be born of water and *of* the Spirit, he cannot enter into the kingdom of God. That which is born of the flesh is flesh; and that which is born of the Spirit is spirit. Marvel not that I said unto thee, 'Ye must be born again'" (John 3:5-7). If we only knew what these words mean to us, to be born of God! An infilling of the life of God, a new life from God, a new creation, living in the world but not of the world, knowing the blessedness of that word, "Sin shall not have dominion over you" (Romans 6:14a).

GOD IN YOU

How shall we reach this place in the Spirit? By the provision of the Holy Spirit that God makes. If we live in the Spirit we shall find all that is carnal swallowed up in life. There is an infilling of the Spirit which quickens our mortal bodies. Give God your life, and you will see that sickness has to go when God comes in fully. Then you are to walk before God, and you will find that he will perfect that which concerns you. That is the place where he wants believers to live, the place where the Spirit of the Lord comes into our whole being. That is the place of victory.

Look at the disciples. Before they received the Holy Spirit, they were in bondage. When Christ said, "One of you shall betray me," they were all doubtful of themselves and questioned, "Is it I?" (Matthew 26:21-22). They were conscious of their human depravity and helplessness. Peter said, "Though I should die with thee, yet will I not deny thee" (vs 35). The others declared the same; yet they all forsook him and fled. But after the power of God fell upon them in the upper room, they were like lions in meeting difficulty. They were bold. What made them so? The purity and power that is by the Spirit.

God can make you an overcomer. When the Spirit of God comes into your surrendered being he transforms you. There is a life in the Spirit that makes you free, and there is an audacity about it, and there is a personality in it. It is God in you. God is able to so transform you and change you, that all the old order has to go before God's new order.

Do you think that God will make you to be a failure? God never made humankind to be a failure. He made us to be a son: to walk the earth in the power of the Spirit, master over the flesh and the devil, until nothing arises within us except that which will magnify and glorify the Lord.

Jesus came to set us free from sin, to free us from sickness, so that we should go forth in the power of the Spirit and minister to the needy, sick, and afflicted. Through the revelation of the Word of God, we find that divine healing is solely for the glory of God, and that salvation is walking in newness of life so that we are inhabited by another, even God.

THE MAN AND HIS MESSAGE

Originally titled "Divine Life Brings Divine Health" from the *Pentecostal Evangel* (Springfield, Missouri), January 17, 1942, page 2. Originally published in *Triumphs of Faith* (Oakland, California), January 1924, pages 5-8. Also published in tract form by Victory Press, North Melbourne, Australia.

People who were close to Smith Wigglesworth were struck by his devotion to the Savior and his spiritually disciplined life. According to his friend George Stormont, he partook of holy communion every day whether he was in church, at home, or some other place. "If other believers were with him, he would share with them. If not, he would partake alone."[1] If during a conversation with friends he sensed he needed to commune with God, he would excuse himself and find a place to pray.

TWELVE

Children of Circumstances or Children of Faith?

In the third chapter of Ephesians, Paul writes of his mission to the Gentiles: "God has grafted us in." In other ages it was not made known that the Gentiles should be fellow heirs of the gospel. Now Paul explains that God made him a minister "by the effectual working of his power" (vs 7).

This power in Paul humbled him to such a degree that he said he was the least of all saints, that to him was given this grace of mystery and revelation. It came forth as a living reality of a living substance indwelling him: "to the intent that now unto the principalities and powers in heavenly *places* might be known by the church the manifold wisdom of God" (vs 10).

This wisdom of God is only revealed in the depths of humiliation where the Holy Ghost has full charge. There alone it is that the vision comes to all his saints. We are now in the process of revelation. You must let the Holy Ghost have his perfect office—a new order of breathing.

First, a calculation of the mind: I can go no further. I give myself to a new order, the manifold wisdom of God, "in whom we have boldness and access with confidence by the faith of him" (vs 12). Boldness brings us into a place of access, confidence, laying hold, taking all off the table and making it ours.

The Holy Ghost in the human body unfolds this age-old mystery that we might know and have the revelation according to the will of God. Paul's flesh was brought to a place of non-existence, that in the life of this man should come out the mighty power of God on our behalf. Paul could get no further. He says, "I bow my knees unto the Father" (vs 14).

WE ARE ALL ONE

Jude also speaks of praying in the Holy Ghost. There is no natural line of thought here, not one point in particular upon which the mind can rest, but that which is predicted from the throne of glory. Then the tongue and all the divine attributes are displayed above all, exceedingly above all, that the glory of God may be revealed in the face of Jesus.

You are his workmanship, created for his glory. God cannot display the greater glory except through those coequal in the glory. The Holy Ghost is the ideal and brings out the very essence of heaven through the human soul. Oh, the need of the baptism of the Holy Ghost! Paul was held in the Spirit: may it be so in our case. There is no difference. He was willing, for all things bound in the spirit. Here we have the greatest liberty that can come to humanity, all the liberty of heaven open, the "family in heaven and earth" (vs 15).

I love the thought that the veil is so thin that the tie is closer than ever: Christ with them, they with us. One is in heaven; one is on earth. What a loftiness, a reverence, a holiness! A wonderful thing is this wedlock and fellowship in the spirit—now an infinite mind of fulfillment and glory.

"Are they not all ministering spirits?" (Hebrews 1:14a). Who can help us as much as those tied with us? As the body is so fitly framed together by the effectual working of his power, we are all one. Nothing separates us, but we look for the appearance of Jesus. He is there in the glory, and the believers who have gone before us are with him. "For the Lord himself shall descend from heaven with a shout,... and the dead in Christ shall rise first: Then we who are alive *and* remain shall be caught up together with them in the clouds, to meet the Lord in the air: and so shall we ever be with the Lord" (1 Thessalonians 4:16-17).

We can only pray as the Holy Ghost gives utterance (Ephesians 3:16). Here the Holy Ghost gives the highest principles through this prayer: that the purposes of salvation are a continuous working and an increasing power. The day that is coming will declare all things. We are strengthened by the Spirit according to the riches of his glory.

FILLED WITH THE GLORY

What is the glory? All the glory that ever comes is from Jesus. You have the glory in the measure that you have the Son of glory in you. If you are filled with Jesus, you are filled with the glory. When you have the spirit of wisdom and revelation in the knowledge of him, there is nothing to hinder the Holy Ghost having control of your whole being.

This happens as by faith: "That Christ may dwell in your hearts by faith" (Ephesians 3:17a). Faith is the production of all things, the Holy Ghost indwelling and enlarging us until the whole body is filled with Christ. And we are coming to that place in a very remarkable way.

Did the Holy Ghost ever utter a prayer that divine power could not answer? In John 17:21, Jesus prayed, "That they all may be one: as thou, Father, *art* in me, and I in thee, that they also may be one in us." What is at work in us as we are one with him, rooted and grounded? *Perfect love.* And perfect love has *justice* wrapped up in it, and the day is coming when the saints will say "amen" to the judgments of God. Justice will do it.

All the wood, hay, and stubble must be destroyed. But rooted and grounded in the Word, I am a production of what God is forming and I can stay the gates of hell and laugh in the face of calamity. I can say, "All things work together for good to them that love God" (Romans 8:28a). Rooted and grounded in love. So-and-so may leave me, but if I am grounded, it is for my good and nothing can be against me but myself.

We live for the glory of God. The Lord, it is he who establishes, strengthens, and upholds, making strong that which is weak and enabling us to stand in the midst of difficulty and in the day of battle. God is with us to do exceedingly above all we can ask or think.

Are we children of circumstances or children of faith? If we are on natural lines, we are troubled at the wind blowing, for as it blows, it whispers fearfulness. But if you are rooted and grounded, you can withstand the tests. And it is only then that you prove what is the breadth and length and depth and height, and know the love of Christ (Ephesians 3:18).

It is an addition sum to meet every missionary's need, to display God's power, enlarging that which needs to be quickened. Breadth: the whole person seeing God as sufficient in every state. The length of things: believing that God is in everything. Oh, the depths! But God is even in the depths! The heights! God is always lifting us up. The revelation to the mind in that one verse is enough to enable anyone in any circumstance to triumph.

We are able to do "exceeding abundantly above all that we ask or think" (vs 20). This is not according to the *mind of Paul* but according to the *revelation of the Spirit.* Filled with all the fulness of God (vs 19). Our natural capacity, when filled with simplicity, has within it an enlargement of itself. But this fulness refers to an ideal power of God in the human soul whereby every part of us is enlarged by the Spirit. God is there to make us full, and we are full as our faith reaches out to the measure: "filled with all the fulness of God."

The power of the Lord was present to heal through his disciples, fulness of power pressed out of them unto others. In Acts 1 we see the power of the Holy Ghost filling Jesus. He became lighter and lighter until he was lifted back to where he was before he took on human flesh: in the presence of God. Jesus Christ manifested in the flesh the power of God in human form, the fulness of the Godhead bodily manifested in Jesus. John said that Jesus was the light of life, increasing in fulness until wafted away entirely, in substance the fulness of God. "Exceeding abundantly above all that we ask or think."

"How can the power of God be fulfilled in me?" you ask. It is filled there in the glory! But it's a tremendous thing! God will have to do something! Beloved, it is not according to your mind at all, but according to the mind of God, according to the revelation of the Spirit. Above all you could ask or think! Verily, not one of us is worthy, but God is worthy! It's above all you can ask! How can it be possible? God puts it in your heart! He can do it!

We have been hearing much about war loans and interest, but if you will follow him, God will add and enlarge and enlarge and lift you all the time, adding compound interest. *Five* percent! No! A *thousand* percent, a *million* percent! If you will, if holiness is the purpose of your heart, it shall be, for God is in his place.

Will you be in his plan of abundance according to the power that works, working in you? Whatever and wherever you are at any time, it will be by God's effectual power: lifting, controlling, carrying you in constant rest and peace. It is according to the power that works in you. "Unto him *be* glory in the church by Christ Jesus throughout all ages, world without end. Amen" (Ephesians 3:21).

THE MAN AND HIS MESSAGE

Originally titled "Exceedingly above All You Can Ask or Think" from *Confidence* (Pittington, Durham), January-March 1918, pages 5-7. A writer who saw Wigglesworth minister to what is now First Assembly, Dallas, in the 1930s described his ministry as uncompromising and one which glorified God: "He gave all the same attention, even though there were over one hundred in line for prayer. One by one, they came, and as they came he would lay hands upon them and always pray, 'in the name of Jesus.'

"One could feel great power there.... He wasn't sensational, no special songs, he did not play a guitar or crack any funny jokes, and yet the people came. A man past his seventies, and yet he arouses Dallas as no other preacher has..... One morning we counted over forty-five pastors and evangelists from the fields; some drove nearly four hundred miles to be there—just to sit and listen to a plumber now filled with the Holy Ghost."[1]

THIRTEEN

Pressing through to Victory

Now, beloved, I believe the Lord wants me to read a few verses from St. Mark's Gospel. Turn to the second chapter. [Here followed the story of the healing of the palsied man, carried by four friends and let down through the housetop at Jesus' feet.] "And immediately he arose, took up the bed, and went forth before them all; insomuch that they were all amazed, and glorified God, saying, 'We never saw it in this fashion'" (Mark 2:12).

Something ought to happen all the time so that people will say, "We never saw anything like that." If there is anything with which God is dissatisfied, it is stationary conditions. So many people stop on the threshold, when God in his great plan is inviting them into his treasury. Oh, this treasury of the Most High, the unsearchable riches of Christ, this divine position into which God wants to move us so that we are altogether new creations.

A TOUCH OF REALITY

You know that the flesh profits nothing. "The carnal mind *is* enmity against God: for it is not subject to the law of God, neither indeed can be" (Romans 8:7). As we cease to live in the old life and know the resurrection power of the Lord, we come into a place of rest, of faith, joy, peace, blessings, and life everlasting. Glory to God!

May the Lord give us a new vision of himself, a fresh touch of divine life and his presence that will shake off all that remains of the old life and bring us fully into his newness of life. May God reveal to us the greatness of his will concerning us, for there is no one who loves us like he does. Yes, beloved, there is no love like his, no compassion like his. He is filled with compassion, and never fails to take those who will fully obey him into the promised land.

You know, beloved, in God's Word there is always more to follow, always more than we know. Oh, if we could only be babies this afternoon, with a childlike mind to take in all the mind of God, what wonderful things would happen! I wonder if you take the Bible just for yourself. It is grand. Never mind who takes only a part; you take it *all*. When you get such a thirst that nothing can satisfy you but God, you shall have a royal time.

The child of God must have reality all the time. After we come into the sweetness of the perfume of the presence of God, we will have the hidden treasures of God and will always be feeding on that blessed truth that will make life full of glory.

Are you dry? There is no dry place in God, but all the good things come out of hard times. The harder the place you are in, the more blessedness can come out of it as you yield to his plan. Oh, if I had only known God's plan in its fulness I might never have had a tear in my life. God is so abundant, so full of love and mercy. There is no lack to those who trust in him.

As I bring you these words this afternoon on the lines of faith, I pray that God may give us some touch of reality, so that we may be able to trust him all the way. It is an ideal thing to get people to believe that when they ask, they shall receive. But how could it be otherwise? It must be so when God says it.

Now we have a beautiful word brought before us this afternoon in the case of this man with the palsy, a helpless man, so infirm that he could not help himself get to the place where Jesus was. Four men, whose hearts were full of compassion, carried the man to the house, but the house was full. Oh, I can see that house today as it was filled, jammed, and crammed—just as we have seen it in Mexico, in Switzerland, in Sweden, in Norway, and in Denmark. The places have been packed to hear the words of our Savior. And it was so at this house in Capernaum. There was no room, even by the door. It was crowded inside and crowded outside.

The men who were carrying the palsied man said, "What shall we do?" But there is always a way. I have never found faith to fail, never once. May the Holy Ghost give us a new touch of faith in God's unlimited power. May we have a living faith that will dare to trust him and say, "Lord, I do believe."

There was no room, "not so much as about the door," but these men said, "Let's climb up onto the housetop." Unbelieving people would say, "Oh, that is silly, ridiculous, foolish!" But these men of faith said, "We must get him in at all costs. It is nothing to move the roof. Let's go up and go through."

Lord, take us today, and let us go through. Let us drop right into the arms of Jesus. It is a lovely place to drop into—out of our self-righteousness, out of our self-consciousness, out of our unbelief. Some people have been in strange places of deadness for years, but God can shake them out of it. Thank God some of the molds have been broken. It is a blessed thing when the old mold gets broken, for God has a new mold. And he can make perfect out of the imperfect by his own loving touch.

I tell you, my sister, my brother, since the day that Christ's blood was shed, since the day of his atonement, he has paid the price to meet all the world's need and its cry of sorrow. Truly Jesus has met the need of the broken hearts and the sorrowful spirits, and also of the withered limbs and the broken bodies. God's dear Son paid the debt for all, for he took our infirmities and bore our sicknesses. In all points he was tempted like as we are, in order that he might be able to succor those who are tempted.

I rejoice to bring him to you today, in a new way it may be in some ways—even though it be in my crooked Yorkshire speech—and say to you that he is the only Jesus; he is the only plan; he is the only life; he is the only help. But thank God he has triumphed to the uttermost. He came to seek and to save that which was lost, and he heals all who come to him.

DROPPING INTO THE ARMS OF JESUS

As the palsied man was let down through the roof, there was a great commotion, and all the people were gazing up at this strange sight. "When Jesus saw their faith, he said unto the sick of the palsy, 'Son, thy sins are forgiven thee'" (Mark 2:5). What had the forgiveness of sins to do with the healing of this man? It had *everything* to do with it. Sin is at the root of disease. May the Lord cleanse us this afternoon from outward sin and from inbred sin, and take away from us all that hinders the power of God to work through us.

The scribes reasoned in their hearts thus, "Who can forgive sins but God only?" (vs 7). But the Lord answered the thoughts of their hearts by saying, "Whether is it easier to say to the sick of the palsy, 'Thy sins be forgiven thee;' or to say, 'Arise, and take up thy bed, and walk?' But that ye may know that the Son of Man hath power on earth to forgive sins,... I say unto thee, 'Arise, and take up thy bed, and go thy way into thine house'" (vs 9-11).

Jesus had seen the weakness of that man, his helplessness. He saw also the faith of his four friends. There is something in this for us today. Many people will not be saved unless some of you are used to stir them up. Remember that you are your brother's keeper. You must take your brother or sister in need to Jesus. When these men carried the palsied man, they pressed through until he could hear the voice of the Son of God, and liberty came to the captive. The man became strong by the power of God, arose, took up his bed, and went forth before them all.

Oh, beloved, I have seen wonderful things like this wrought by the power of God. We must never think about our God on small lines. He spoke the Word one day and made the world of things that had not been. That is the kind of God we have, and he is just the same today. There is no change in him. He is lovely and precious above all thought and comparison. There is none like him.

I am certain today that nothing will profit you but that which you take by faith. God wants you to come into a close place with him where you will believe and claim the promises, for they are "yes" and "amen" to all who believe. Let us thank God for this full gospel which is not hidden under a bushel today.

Let us thank the Lord that he is bringing out the gospel as in the days of his flesh. God is all the time working right in the very midst of us, but I want to know, what are *you* going to do with the gospel today? There are greater blessings for you than you have ever received in your life. Do you believe it and will you receive it?

THE MAN AND HIS MESSAGE

Originally titled "Pressing Through" from *Triumphs of Faith* (Oakland, California), September 1922, pages 208-11. A message delivered at Carrie Judd Montgomery's Monday Meeting, Danish Hall, Oakland, California, and reported by Miss Mabel Bingham.

"Pressing through" could very well be the plumber-preacher's motto, and with a little imagination, we can see him as one of the men who carried the palsied man to Jesus. As Wigglesworth overcame early difficulties in his own life, he was able to understand and help others. "[His] personal road to triumph in the supernatural realm was a hard, rocky path of brokenness, failure, and deeper submission to the ways of God," David Dories noted. "Yet he never quit. His persistent hungering and spiritual victory kept him pressing forward for more. As the baptism in the Spirit plunged him into a much greater measure of joy and power than he had known previously, he was moved by a heavy burden of compassion for fellow believers who lived in continual bondage to condemnation and defeat."[1]

FOURTEEN

Doing the Works of Jesus

Tonight we will be looking at the fourteenth chapter of John's Gospel, taking verses twelve to fourteen for our lesson. Jesus is speaking, and the Spirit can take the words of our Lord Jesus and make them as real to us as if he were speaking here tonight. He says, "Verily, verily, I say unto you, He that believeth on me, the works that I do shall he do also; and greater *works* than these shall he do; because I go unto my Father. And whatsoever ye shall ask in my name, that will I do, that the Father may be glorified in the Son. If ye shall ask any thing in my name, I will do *it.*"

Look at this promise: "He that believeth on me... greater *works* than these shall he do." What a word! Is it true? If you want truth, where will you get it? "Your Word is truth," Jesus said to the Father. When you take up God's Word, you get the truth. God is not the author of confusion or error. Rather his Word enlightens and brings forth that which reveals truth unto us like the noonday. It changes us, and we enter into fellowship, into communion, into faith, into assurance, into God's likeness, for we saw the truth and believed.

I see that faith is an operative power. God opens the understanding of our hearts and shows us things we would never have known otherwise. I do not think we have greater words than these written in Romans 4:16: "Therefore *it is* of faith, that *it might be* by grace." Grace is God's benediction coming right down to you. And when you open the door to him—which is an act of faith—he does all you want. It is by faith that it might be by grace. You are the one to open the way; God is the one to replenish your need all along the way.

Our Lord Jesus comes to us and says, "You have seen me work and how I work." Did anyone ever work as Jesus did? I do not mean his carpentering. No. He worked in the hearts of the people. He drew them to him. They came with their needs, with their depressions, and he relieved them all. This royal visitor, who came from the Father to express his love, talked to people, spent time with them in their homes, and most likely lodged with some of them overnight.

This worker of miracles said, "You see what I have been doing: healing the sick, relieving the oppressed, casting out demons. The works that I do shall you do also." Dare you believe? Will you take up the work Jesus left and carry it on? "He who believes on me." What is this? What does it mean? How can just believing bring to pass these things? What virtue is there in it? It is because Jesus said it. If we will take it up and also say it, it shall be accomplished in our lives.

"He that believeth... greater *works* than these shall he do" (John 14:12). But unbelief has hindered our progress in both our human activity and our divine activity. We must put away unbelief. Open your heart to God's grace, and he will come and place in you a definite faith. He wants to move every obstruction from before you. By the grace of God, I want to so establish you that when you go out of this place, whatever comes across your path, you can rise with divine power to rebuke and destroy it.

Faith is a matter of definite and clear understanding between

God and us. We come to see that Jesus has a life force to put in us that changes everything that we dare to believe. "He who believes that Jesus is the Christ overcomes the world." Because we believe that Jesus is the Christ, the essence of divine life in us by faith causes a perfect separation between us and the world. We have no room for sin. It is joyful for us to be doing that which is right. This is a divine revelation.

As with sin in the world, so it is with sickness and afflictions in the world, both in us and in others. For the one who believes—who dares to believe, who dares to trust—it will come to pass.

HAS GOD FORGOTTEN HOW?

A woman said to me one night, "Can I hear again? Is it possible for me to ever hear again? I have had several operations, and the drums of my ears removed." I said, "If God has not forgotten how to make drums for ears, you can hear again."

Do you think God has forgotten? What does God forget? He forgets our sins. "When he forgives, he forgets," as the song goes. But he has not forgotten how to make eardrums. When I was in Melbourne five years ago a woman told me that her lungs were in ribbons and that she could part with a pint of puss anytime. God squared up that woman at one meeting.

Not very long ago, the power of God was very much on the meeting, and I was telling the people that they could be healed without my going to them. If they would rise up, I would pray and the Lord would heal. There was a man who put up his hands. I said, "Can't that man rise?" They said he could not and lifted him up. And so I prayed that God would restore his strength.

When it was manifest that this man was healed—that his ribs which had been broken and not joined were healed—there was such faith in the place that a young girl said, "Please, gentleman, come to me. Please come to me." You could not see her, she was so small. The mother said, "My daughter wants you to come." So I went over to this girl who was about fourteen years old. She said, with tears streaming down her face, "Will you pray for me?" "Dare you believe?" I asked. "Oh, yes," she answered right away. The meeting had made me long for Jesus, I was so moved. I prayed and placed my hands on her head in the name of Jesus.

"Mother," the girl said, "I am being healed. Take those things off. Take them all off." She had straps on her legs and an iron brace on her foot about three and a half inches thick, and asked her mother to unstrap them all. The mother loosed straps and bands, and then the daughter said, "Mother, I am sure I am healed." There were not many people with dry eyes as they saw that girl walk about with legs quite as true as when she was born. God healed her right away.

What did it? "Please, gentleman, come to me," she had said, her longing coupled with faith. I come to you tonight. I see that we can be as little children. God has hidden these things from the wise and prudent, but revealed them to babes. There is something in a childlike faith in God that makes us dare to believe. I want you to know that whatever there is in your life that is bound, that the name of Jesus—the power of the name—shall break it if you believe.

Jesus says, "Whatsoever ye shall ask in my name, that will I do it" (John 14:13). And he says, "When I do it God will be so pleased that he will be glorified in me." God will be glorified in Jesus when you receive life and freedom from Jesus through your faith. God grant unto you tonight, God breathe through you tonight, God help you tonight to take your stand for him. Dare to believe.

I believe I have before me men and women of intellect who long that God should use them. Do you think that the truth could come tonight to mock you? Don't you see that God really means that you should live in the world to relieve the oppression of the world? That is why God has brought us together: to be quickened, to be molded afresh, that the Word of God may change everything that needs to be changed—both in us and for others as we dare to believe and command it to be done.

THE MAN AND HIS MESSAGE

Originally titled "Dare to Believe, then Command" from the *Pentecostal Evangel* (Springfield, Missouri), April 9, 1927, pages 1, 8-9, reprinted from the *Australian Evangel.*

Before Wigglesworth preached this sermon in Melbourne, he stopped in Sydney to conduct meetings scheduled in a Baptist church. The minister had agreed to invite the English evangelist to preach on the recommendation of one of his deacons, without knowing that he was pentecostal and prayed for the sick. "To say that this pentecostal evangelist caused a stir would be a prime understatement. The reaction to his forceful ministry, with his doctrine and demonstration, was revolutionary. The minister and his deacons immediately cancelled his meetings in the church, but not before Smith Wigglesworth had prophesied that the minister and the church knew not the day of their visitation."[1] With that door firmly closed in his face, Wigglesworth went on to hold a very successful month-long crusade in a large auditorium in Sydney.

FIFTEEN

Be Not Afraid, Only Believe

I want to read one of those marvelous truths of the Scriptures that was written to help us to believe God: "Be not afraid, only believe" (Mark 5:36). It is our privilege not only to enter in by faith but also to become partakers of the blessing God wants to give us.

My message is on the lines of faith. Because some do not hear in faith, it profits them nothing. There is a hearing of faith, and there is a hearing which means nothing more than listening to words. I beseech you to see to it that everything done may bring not only blessing to you but strength and character, and that you may be able to see the goodness of God in this meeting. I have many things to relate about people who dared to believe God until it came to pass.

I want to impress upon you the importance of believing what the Scripture says. This is a wonderful Word, an everlasting Word, a Word of power, a Word of health, a Word of substance, a Word of life. It breathes life into our very nature, to all of us who lay hold of it, if we believe.

I want you to understand that there is a need for the Word of God. But it is precisely a *need*, many times, that brings us the blessing. Why am I here? Because God delivered me when no other hand could do it. I stand before you as one who was given up by everybody, when no one could help. I was earnest and zealous for the salvation of souls. If you were in Bradford, you would know. We had police protection for nearly twenty years in the best thoroughfare in the city. And in my humble way, along with my dear wife who was all on fire for God, we were daily ministering in the open air.

Full of zeal? Yes. But one night, thirty years ago, I was carried home helpless. We knew very little about divine healing, but we prayed through to victory. It is thirty years and more since God healed me. I am now sixty-eight years old and fresher, in better health, and more fit for work than I was at that time. It is a most wonderful experience when the life of God becomes the life of a human being. The divine power that sweeps through the organism, cleansing the blood, makes that man or woman fresh every day. The life of God is resurrection power.

GOD ALONE

I will tell you an incident that happened in Switzerland that will stir up your faith. After I had been preaching there for some weeks, a brother worker said, "Will you not go to the meeting tonight?" "No," I said, "I have been at it all this time. Can you take charge tonight?"

"What shall we do?" he asked. "Do?" I said. "Paul the apostle left people to do the work and passed on to another place. I have been here long enough now; *you* do the work." So this man of faith went to the meeting. When he came back he said, "We have had a wonderful time." "What happened?" I asked. He said, "I invited them all out, took off my coat, and rolled up my sleeves and prayed, and they were all healed. I did just like you did."

Jesus told his disciples, "I give you power over all the power of the enemy." They entered into the houses and healed the sick therein. This ministry of divine operation in us is wonderful, but who would take upon themselves to say, "I can do this or that"? If it is *God*, it is all right; but if it is *ourselves*, it is all wrong.

When you are weak, then you are strong. When you are strong in your own strength, you are weak. You must realize this truth and live only in the place where the power of God rests upon you, and where the Spirit moves within you. Then God will mightily manifest his power and you will know, as Jesus said, "The Spirit of the Lord is upon me."

God brings a remarkable, glorious fact to our minds tonight in this fifth chapter of Mark: the healing of a little, helpless girl. The physicians had failed. The mother said to the father, "There is only one hope: if you can see Jesus! As sure as you can meet Jesus, our daughter will live." Do you think it is possible for anybody anywhere to go looking for Jesus without seeing him? Is it possible to think about Jesus without his drawing near? No. This man knew the power there was in the name of Jesus: "In my name shall you cast out devils."

But we must be sure we know that name, for in Acts 19 the seven sons of Sceva said to the man possessed by devils: "We adjure you by Jesus whom Paul preacheth [to come out]" (vs 13). The evil spirit said, "Jesus I know, and Paul I know; but who are ye?" (vs 15). Yes, the devil knows every believer. And the seven sons of Sceva nearly lost their lives. The evil powers came upon them and they barely escaped.

The power is more than repeating the name; it is the nature of the name in you. It is the divine personality within, who has come to take up his abode in you. And when he becomes all in all, then God works through you. It is the life, the power of God. God works through the life. The Lord is that life and the ministry of it. And the power in that ministry by the Holy Spirit brings everybody into such a place of divine relationship that Jesus mightily lives in us and enables us to overcome the powers of the enemy.

The Lord healed that child as they got a vision of Jesus. The word of the Lord came not with observation but with divine, mighty power, working in them; until by the power of the Spirit, men and women were created anew by this new life divine. We have to see that when this divine Word comes to us by the power of the Holy Ghost, it is according to the will of God that we speak; not with human wisdom, but with divine minds operated by the Word of God; not as channels only, but as oracles of the Spirit.

JESUS SPOKE WITH AUTHORITY

As the ruler of the synagogue sought Jesus, he worshiped him. How they gathered around him! How everybody listened to what he had to say! Jesus spoke not as a scribe, but with authority and power, his words decked with divine glory.

A young man who was preaching in a marketplace was confronted by some atheists. "There have been five Christs," they said. "Tell us which one it is that you preach." He answered, "The Christ who rose from the dead." There is only one who rose from the dead. There is only one Jesus who lives. And as he lives, we live also. Glory to God! We are risen with him, are living with him, and will reign with him.

This ruler, as he drew near the crowd, went up to Jesus and said, "My little daughter lieth at the point of death: *I pray thee,* come and lay thy hands on her, that she may be healed" (Mark 5:23). "I will come," Jesus said. What a beautiful assurance. But as they were coming along the road, a woman met them who had been suffering an issue of blood for twelve years. When this trouble began, she sought many physicians. Now she had no more money because the physicians had taken it all and left her worse than they found her.

Have you any doctors who do the same thing around here? When I was a plumber, I had to finish my work before I got the money—and I didn't always get it then! I think that if there were an arrangement whereby no doctor received his fee until he cured the patient, there wouldn't be so many people who die.

Twelve years of sickness this woman had endured. She needed someone now who could heal her *without* money, for she was bankrupt and helpless. Jesus comes to people who are withered, diseased, lame, crippled in all kinds of ways. And when he comes he proclaims liberty to the captive, opening of eyes to the blind, and the opening of ears to the deaf.

Many people must have said to this woman, "If you had only been with us today. We saw the most marvelous things—the crooked made straight, the lame to walk, the blind to see." And the woman who had been sick for twelve years might have replied, "Oh, you make me feel that if I could only see him I should be healed." It strengthened her faith and it became firm. She had a purpose within her.

Faith is a mighty power; faith will reach everything. When real faith comes into operation, you will not say, "I don't feel much better." Faith says, "I am whole." Faith doesn't say, "It's a lame leg"; faith says, "My leg is all right." Faith never sees a goiter either. A young woman with a goiter came for prayer. In a testimony meeting she said, "I do praise the Lord for healing my goiter." She went home and said to her mother, "Oh, Mother, when the man prayed for me, God healed my goiter."

For twelve months she went about telling everybody how God had healed her goiter. After that year had passed, I was in the same place and people said, "How big that lady's goiter is!" The time came for a testimony. She jumped up and said, "I was here twelve months ago and God healed me of my goiter. Such a marvelous twelve months!" When this woman returned home her folks said, "You should have seen the people today when you testified that God had healed your goiter. They think there is something wrong with you. If you go upstairs and look in the mirror, you will see that your goiter is bigger than ever."

This woman of faith went upstairs, but she didn't look in the mirror. Instead, she got down on her knees and said, "Oh, Lord, let all the people know, just as you have let me know, how wonderfully you have healed me." The next morning her neck was as perfect as any neck you ever saw. Faith never looks. Faith praises God, and it is done!

This poor, helpless woman in Mark 5 who had been sick for twelve years had been growing weaker and weaker. She pushed into the crowded thoroughfare when she knew Jesus was in their midst. She was stirred to the depths, and she pushed through and touched him. If you will believe God and touch him, you will be healed at once. Jesus is the healer!

Now listen! Some people put the touch of the Lord in the place of faith. The Lord would not have that woman believe that the *touch* had done it. She felt as soon as she touched him that healing power had gone through her, which is true. When the Israelites were bitten by fiery serpents in the wilderness, God said through Moses, "He who looks upon this serpent of brass shall be healed" (see Numbers 21). The look made it possible for God to do it.

Did the touch heal the woman? No. The touch meant something more: it demonstrated a living faith. Jesus said, "Thy *faith* hath made thee whole" (Mark 5:34a). If God would just move on us to believe, there wouldn't be a sick person who could not receive healing. But beware: as soon as this woman who had been healed began to testify with all the crowd about her, the devil came. The devil is always in a testimony meeting. When the sons of God gathered together in the time of Job, he was there.

While this was happening in the street, three people came running from the house of Jairus and said, "There is no use now. Your daughter is dead. This Jesus can do nothing for a dead daughter. Your wife needs you at home." But Jesus said, "Be not afraid. Only believe."

He speaks the word just in time! Jesus is never behind time. When the tumult is the worst, the pain the most severe, the cancer gripping the body, then the word comes, "Only believe." When everything seems as though it will fail and is practically hopeless, the Word of God comes to us, "Only believe."

When Jesus came to the ruler's house he found a lot of people weeping and wailing. He said, "Why make ye this ado and weep? The damsel is not dead, but sleepeth" (Mark 5:39). There is a wonderful word that God wants you to hear. Jesus said, "I am the resurrection, and the life" (John 11:25a). The believer may fall asleep, but the believer doesn't die. Oh, that people would understand the deep things of God, it would change the whole situation. It makes you look out with a glorious hope to the day when the Lord shall come.

What does Scripture say? "Those who sleep will God bring with him." Jesus knew that. "The damsel is not dead, but sleepeth. And they laughed him to scorn" (Mark 5:39-40a). To show the insincerity of these wailers, they could turn from wailing to laughing. Jesus took the father and the mother of the maid and, going into the room where she was, took her hand and said, "Damsel, I say unto thee, arise" (vs 41). And the child sat up. Praise the Lord! And Jesus said, "Give her something to eat."

Oh, what a remarkable Lord Jesus! I want to impress upon you the importance of realizing that he is in our midst. No person need be without the knowledge that they are not only saved but that God can live in these human bodies. You are begotten unto a lively hope the moment you believe.

"He who believes has eternal life." You have eternal life the moment you believe. The first life is temporal, natural, material, but in the new birth you exist as long as God wills—forever. We are begotten by an incorruptible power, by the Word of God. The new birth is unto righteousness, begotten by God the moment that we believe. God always saves through the heart. He who believes in his heart and confesses with his mouth shall be saved.

Jesus is here tonight to loose those who are bound. If you are suffering in your body, he will heal you now as we pray. He is saying to every sin-sick soul, to every disease-smitten one, "Be not afraid, only believe."

THE MAN AND HIS MESSAGE

From the *Pentecostal Evangel* (Springfield, Missouri), July 16, 1927, pages 1, 6-7. Wigglesworth gives his testimony of healing thirty years previous and adds, "I am sixty-eight years old and fresher, in better health, and more fit for work than I was at that time." He remained active in the ministry for another twenty years.

After the evangelist's death on March 12, 1947, missionary James Salter wrote this tribute to his father-in-law: "When he commenced his healing ministry, he was officially and publicly derided by many of his old friends, but as the years went by he was able to heap coals of fire on their heads by ministering to their needy bodies. Many who had scorned and scoffed publicly later sought him privately and at nighttime for the blessing of the effectual and fervent prayers of a righteous man."

Salter added that every mail delivery brought testimonies of people who had read *Ever-Increasing Faith.* "In every country its simple and sufficient message 'only believe' has linked tens of thousands of people to the living, saving, healing, victorious Lord Jesus."[1]

PART THREE:

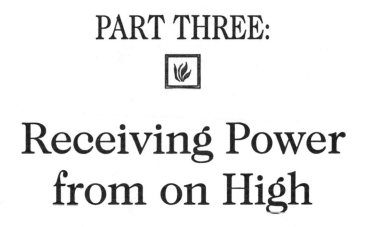

Receiving Power from on High

SIXTEEN

The Resurrection Touch

We have a remarkable word from John the Baptist in Matthew 3:11: "I indeed baptize you with water unto repentance: but he that cometh after me is mightier than I, whose shoes I am not worthy to bear: he shall baptize you with the Holy Ghost, and *with* fire."

This was the word of one who was filled with the Holy Ghost even from his mother's womb, who was so filled with the power of the Spirit of God that people came from east and west and from north and south to the banks of the Jordan to hear him. You have seen water baptism, and you know what it means. This later baptism taught by this wilderness preacher means that we shall be so immersed, covered, and flooded with the blessed Holy Ghost that he fills our whole body.

Now let us see what Jesus said about this experience in John 7:37-39: "In the last day, that great *day* of the feast, Jesus stood and cried saying, 'If any man thirst, let him come unto me, and drink. He that believeth on me, as the scripture hath said, out of his belly shall flow rivers of living water.' (But this spake he of the Spirit, which they that believe on him should receive: for the Holy Ghost was not yet *given;* because that Jesus was not yet glorified.)"

Jesus saw that the people who had come to the feast of Pentecost expecting blessing were going back dissatisfied. He had come to help the needy, to bring satisfaction to the unsatisfied. He does not want any of us to be thirsty, famished, naked, full of discord, full of disorder, full of evil, full of carnality, full of sensuality. And so he sends out in his own blessed way the old prophetic cry: "Ho, every one that thirsteth, come ye to the waters, and he that hath no money; come ye, buy, and eat" (Isaiah 55:1a).

The Master can give you that which will satisfy. He has in himself just what you need at this hour. He knows your greatest need. You need the blessed Holy Ghost, not merely to satisfy your thirst, but to satisfy the needs of thirsty ones everywhere. For as the blessed Holy Spirit flows through you like rivers of living water, these floods will break what needs to be broken. They will bring to death that which should be brought to death, but they will bring life and fruit where there is none.

What do you have? A well of water? That is good as far as it goes. But Christ wants to see a plentiful supply of the river of the Holy Ghost flowing through you. Here, on this last day of the feast, we find him preparing them for the pentecostal fulness that was to come, the fulness that he would shed forth from the glory after his ascension.

A NECESSARY CONDITION

Note the condition necessary: "He that believeth on me." This is the root of the matter. Believe on him. Believing on him will bring forth this river of blessedness. Abraham believed God, and we are all blessed through faithful Abraham. As we believe God, many will be blessed through *our* faith as well. Abraham was an extraordinary man of faith. He believed God in the face of everything. And so God wants to bring *us* to the place of believing—where despite all contradictions, we are strong in faith, giving God glory. As we fully believe God, he will be glorified, and we will prove a blessing to the whole world as was our father Abraham.

In John 14 we see the promise that ignorant and unlearned fishermen were to be clothed with the Spirit, anointed with power from on high, and endued with the Spirit of wisdom and knowledge. As God imparts divine wisdom, you will not act foolishly. The Spirit of God will give you a sound mind, and he will impart to you the divine nature.

How could these weak and helpless fishermen, poor and needy, ignorant and unlearned, do the works of Christ and greater works than he had done? They were humanly incapable. None of us is able. But our emptiness has to be clothed with divine fulness, and our helplessness has to be filled with the power of God's helpfulness. Paul knew this when he gloried in all that brought him down in weakness, for flowing into his weakness came a mighty deluge of divine power.

Christ knew that his going away would leave his disciples like a family of orphans. But he told them it was expedient, it was best, for after his return to the Father, Jesus would send the Comforter, and he himself would come to indwell them. "Ye in me, and I in you" (John 14:20b). Christ said, "And I will pray the Father, and he shall give you another Comforter, that he may abide with you for ever; *Even* the Spirit of truth" (John 14:16-17a). What a fitting name for the one who was coming to them at the time they were bereft—Comforter. After Christ had left them, they felt a great need, but that need was met on the day of Pentecost when the Comforter came.

You will always find that in the moment of need the Holy Spirit is a comforter. When my dear wife was lying dead, the doctors could do nothing. They said to me, "She's gone; we cannot help you." My heart was so moved that I said, "Oh,

God, I cannot spare her!" I went up to her and said, "Oh, come back, come back, and speak to me! Come back, come back!"

The Spirit of the Lord moved, and she came back and smiled again. But then the Holy Ghost said to me, "She's mine. Her work is done. She is mine." Oh, that comforting word! No one else could have spoken it. The Comforter came. From that moment my dear wife never regained consciousness. And in this day the Comforter has a word for every bereaved believer.

Christ further said, "But the Comforter, *which is* the Holy Ghost, whom the Father will send in my name, he shall teach you all things, and bring all things to your remembrance, whatsoever I have said unto you" (John 14:26). How true this is. From time to time he takes of the words of Christ and makes them life to us. And, empowered with this blessed Comforter, the words that we speak under the anointing are spirit and life.

AS AT THE BEGINNING

There are some who come to our meetings who, when you ask them whether they are seekers, reply, "Oh, I am ready for anything." I tell them, "Then you will never get anything." It is necessary to have the purpose that the psalmist had when he said, "One *thing* have I desired of the Lord, that will I seek after" (Psalm 27:4). When the Lord reveals to you that you must be filled with the Holy Ghost, seek that one thing until God gives you that gift.

I spoke to two young preachers in a meeting one day, men who had received their divinity degrees. I said to them, "Young men, what about it?" "Oh," they said, "we do not believe in receiving the Holy Ghost in the same way as you people do." I said to them, "You are dressed up like preachers, and it is a pity having to have the dress without the presence." "Well, we do not believe it the way you do," they said.

"But look," I said, "the apostles believed it that way. Wouldn't you like to be like the apostles? You have read how they received at the beginning, haven't you?" Always remember this, that the baptism will always be as at the beginning. It has not changed. If you want a real baptism, expect it just the same way as they had it at the beginning.

These preachers asked, "*What* had they at the beginning?" I quoted from the tenth chapter of Acts where it says, "On the Gentiles also was poured out the gift of the Holy Ghost. For they heard them speak with tongues, and magnify God" (Acts 10:45b-46). The Jewish believers knew that these Gentiles had the same kind of experience as they themselves had on the day of Pentecost.

The experience has not changed; it is still the same as at the beginning. When these two young men realized that Peter and John and the rest of the disciples had received the mighty endowment at the beginning, and that it was for them, they walked up to the front where folk were tarrying. They were finely dressed, but in about half an hour they looked different. They had been prostrated. I had not caused them to do it. But they had been so lost and so controlled by the power of God, and were so filled with the glory of God, that they just rolled over, and their fine clothes were soiled—but their faces were radiant.

What caused the change? They had received what the 120 received at the beginning. These young preachers had been ordained by men. Now they had received an ordination that was better. The Lord had ordained them that they should go and bring forth much fruit. The person who receives this ordination goes forth with fresh feet, his feet shod with the preparation of the gospel of peace. He goes forth with a fresh voice which speaks as the Spirit gives utterance. He goes forth with a fresh mind, a mind illuminated by the power of God. He goes forth with a fresh vision and sees all things new.

When I was in Switzerland, a woman came to me and said, "Now that I am healed and have been delivered from that terrible carnal oppression that bound and fettered me, I feel that I have a new mind. I should like to receive the Holy Ghost, but when I hear these people at the altar making so much noise, I feel like running away."

Shortly after this we were in another place in Switzerland where there was a great hotel joined to the building where we were ministering. At the close of one of the morning services, the power of God fell. That is the only way I can describe it—the power of God fell. This same poor, timid creature, who could not bear to hear any noise, screamed so loud that all the waiters in this big hotel came out—still wearing their aprons and carrying their trays—to see what was up. Nothing especially was "up." Rather, something had come down, and it so altered the situation that this woman could stand anything after that.

FACT, NOT FEELING

When you receive the baptism, remember the words in 1 John 2:20: "Ye have an unction from the Holy One." God grant that we may not forget that truth. Many people, instead of standing on the rock of faith and believing they have received this anointing, say, "Oh, if I could only *feel* the anointing!"

Beloved, your feeling robs you of your greatest anointing. Your feelings are often on the line of discouragement. You have to get away from the walk by sense, for God has said, "The just shall live by his faith" (Habakkuk 2:4b; Romans 1:17b). Believe what God says, "Ye have an unction from the Holy One," an anointing from above. All thoughts of holiness, all thoughts of purity, all thoughts of power are from above.

Frequently I see a condition of emergency. Here is a woman dying; here is a man who has lost all the powers of his faculties; here is a person apparently in death. God does not want me to be filled with anxiety. What does he want me to do? To believe only. After you have received, only believe. Dare to believe the one who has declared, "I will do it." Christ says, "Verily I say unto you, That whosoever shall say unto this mountain, 'Be thou removed, and be thou cast into the sea'; and shall not doubt in his heart, but shall believe that those things which he saith shall come to pass; he shall have whatsoever he saith" (Mark 11:23).

God declares, "You have an anointing." Believe God and you will see this happen. What you say will come to pass. Speak the word and the bound shall be free, the sick shall be healed. "He shall have whatsoever he says." You have an anointing. The anointing has come; the anointing abides; the anointing is with us.

But what if you have not lived in the place where the anointing can be increased? What is the matter? Is there something between you and the Holy One—some uncleanness, some impurity, some desire that is not of him, something that has come in the way? Then the Spirit is grieved. Has the anointing left? No. When he comes in, he comes to abide. Make confession of your sin, of your failure, and once more the precious blood of Jesus Christ will cleanse, and the grieved Spirit will once more manifest himself.

John further says, "The anointing which ye have received of him abideth in you" (1 John 2:27a). We have an anointing, the same anointing which Jesus Christ himself received. For "God anointed Jesus of Nazareth with the Holy Ghost and with power: who went about doing good" (Acts 10:38a). This same anointing is for us.

It means much to have a continuous faith for the manifestation of the anointing. At the death of Lazarus, when it seemed that Mary and Martha and all around them had lost faith, Jesus turned to the Father and said, "Father, I thank thee that thou hast heard me. And I knew that thou hearest me always" (John 11:41b-42a). In the face of such supreme faith that counted on God, that counted on his anointing, death had to give up Lazarus.

Through a constant fellowship with the Father, through bold

faith in the Son, through a mighty anointing of the blessed Holy Spirit, there will come a right of way for God to be enthroned in our hearts, purifying us so thoroughly that there is no room for anything but the divine presence within. And through the manifestation of this presence, the works of Christ and greater works shall be accomplished for the glory of our triune God.

THE MAN AND HIS MESSAGE

Originally titled "Power from on High" from the *Pentecostal Evangel* (Springfield, Missouri), May 27, 1944, pages 2-4. While the nations were being blown apart with bombs and cannon power during World War II, this sermon addresses another power: the power of the Holy Spirit. Wigglesworth taught that this power is available to all believers and comes through faith in God's Word.

During a union pentecostal meeting in Chicago, October 29-November 12, 1922, a Christian magazine editor quoted him on the Word of God: "Never compare this Book with other books. Comparisons are dangerous. Other books are of earth; this is of heaven. Never say that this Book contains the Word of God. It is the Word of God. Eternal in duration; incomprehensible in power; infinite in scope; human in penmanship; present in application. Read it through; write it down. Pray it in! Work it out! Pass it on!"[1]

SEVENTEEN

Filled with New Wine

It is a settled thing in heaven that the latter rain is greater than the former rain (Joel 2:28; Acts 2:16-18). Some of our hearts have been greatly moved by the former rain, but it is the latter rain we are crying for. What will it be like when the time comes and the heart of God is satisfied? We remember what happened on the day of Pentecost: "And they began to speak with other tongues, as the Spirit gave them utterance" (Acts 2:4).

What a lovely thought that the words they spoke were from the Holy Ghost! We are having to learn—whether we like it or not—that when we come to our end, God is only beginning. Then it is all God, and the Lord Jesus stands forth in the midst with such divine glory that we are impelled, filled, led so perfectly. Nothing else will meet the need of the world.

There is something beautiful about how the people in Jerusalem recognized that Peter and John had been with Jesus. There was something so real in these disciples, so much like their Master: "Now when they saw the boldness of Peter and John, and perceived that they were unlearned and ignorant

141

men, they marvelled; and they took knowledge of them, that they had been with Jesus" (Acts 4:13). May all in the temple glorify Jesus; it can be so.

The outstanding thing in the life of Jesus, more than anything else, was the fact that the people glorified God in him. When God is glorified and gets the right of way and the minds of his people, the people are as he is, filled with God. Whatever it costs, it must be. Let it be so. Filled with God!

The only thing to help people is to tell them the latest thing God has given us from the glory. There is nothing outside salvation. We are filled, immersed, clothed; there must be nothing felt, seen, spoken about, but the mighty power of the Holy Ghost. We are new creatures in Christ Jesus, baptized into a new nature. "He that believeth on me . . . out of his belly shall flow rivers of living water" (John 7:38). The very life of the risen Christ in everything, moving us to do his will.

PARTAKERS OF THE DIVINE NATURE

There is something that we have not yet reached, but praise God for the thirst I sense in this meeting! For the thirst is of God, the desire is of God, the plan is of God, the purpose is of God. God's plan, God's thought, God's vessel, and God's servant. We are in the world to meet the need, but not of the world or its spirit. God incarnate in humanity. We become partakers of the divine nature to manifest the life of Jesus to the world.

The world misunderstands, just as they did on the day of Pentecost: "Others mocking said, 'These men are full of new wine'" (Acts 2:13). That is what we want, you say? New wine. A new order, a new inspiration, a new manifestation. New, new, new, new wine. A power all new of itself, as if you were born, as you are, into a new day, a new creation.

It has a freshness about it! It has a beauty about it! It has a quality about it! It will create in others the desire for the same taste as the three thousand felt, tasted, and enjoyed. Some looked on. Others drank with a new faith never before seen—a new manifestation, a new realization all divine. A new thing, straight from heaven, from the throne of the glorified Lord. It is God's mind to fill us with that wine, to make us ready to burst forth with new rivers, fresh energy, no tired feeling.

God manifest in the flesh: that is what we want, and it is what God wants, and it satisfies everybody. All the people said, "We have never seen anything like it." The disciples rejoiced in it being new. Others were brokenhearted, crying out "unto Peter and to the rest of the apostles, 'Men *and* brethren, what shall we do?' Then Peter said unto them, 'Repent, and be baptized, every one of you in the name of Jesus Christ for the remission of sins, and ye shall receive the gift of the Holy Ghost. For the promise is unto you, and to your children, and to all that are afar off, *even* as many as the Lord our God shall call.' And with many other words did he testify and exhort, saying, 'Save yourselves from this untoward generation'" (Acts 2:37-40).

What shall we do? Brothers and sisters, what shall we do? Believe! Stretch out! Press on! Let there be a new entering in, a new passion to have it. We must be beside ourselves; we must drink deeply of the new wine so that multitudes may find satisfaction too.

The new wine is to have a new bottle—the necessity of a new vessel.[1] If anything of the old life is left, not put to death and destroyed, there will be a rending and a breaking. The new wine and the old bottle will not work in harmony. It must be new wine and a new wineskin, then there will be nothing to drop off when Jesus comes. "For the Lord himself shall descend from heaven with a shout, with the voice of the archangel, and with the trump of God: and the dead in Christ shall rise first: Then we which are alive *and* remain shall be caught up together with them in the clouds, to meet the Lord in the air: and so shall we ever be with the Lord" (1 Thessalonians 4:16-17).

When the Spirit is in control of our bodies, the bodies change until we will be like him. "Who shall change our vile body, that it may be fashioned like unto his glorious body, according to the working whereby he is able even to subdue all things unto himself" (Philippians 3:21). I desire you to be all so filled with the Spirit at this convention, so hungry, so thirsty, that nothing will satisfy you but seeing Jesus. Getting thirstier every day, drier every day, until the floods come, and the Master passes by.

Christ will minister to us and through us his life, his inspiration for a hurting world. His death on the cross was painful, but he accomplished the purpose for which he came. "It is finished" (John 19:30), he cried. Let the cry never stop until the heart of Jesus is satisfied, until the earth is filled with the knowledge of the glory of the Lord as the waters cover the sea. Amen. Amen. Amen.

THE MAN AND HIS MESSAGE

From *Confidence* (Sunderland, England), April-June 1918, pages 27, 31-32. Wigglesworth preached this sermon at his annual Easter convention at Bradford. Despite the hardships of World War I, some in attendance described the meeting as "a thousand times in advance of last year." Wigglesworth himself wrote, "A prayer came forth from all to God for our poor, broken world, in its present chaos of war, and a cry was raised for deliverance for our land."

Although he is best known for his healing services, Wigglesworth possibly focused as much attention on hungering for God as he did on healing. "I would rather have a man on my platform, not filled with the Holy Ghost but hungry for God, than a man who has received the Holy Ghost but has become satisfied with his experience."[2]

EIGHTEEN

The Place of Power

The thought that has been pressing upon my mind for some time is the thought of "abiding," the joy of being at that place where I can always count upon being in the presence of power. There I know God's presence is with me, leading to a place where victory is assured. Let us get hold of this thought: that if we keep in a certain place with God, wonderful things may happen, for we shall then be in a place where we reach such spiritual attainment that marvels may be wrought. Then God will have his own way through us.

In the fourth chapter of Luke, first verse, we read, "And Jesus being full of the Holy Ghost returned from the Jordan and was led by the Spirit into the wilderness." Mark speaks about his being "driven" by the Spirit. Whatever Mark means or Luke means, there is one thing certain: we see a power, a majesty, falling on the Lord Jesus. He is no longer the same man. He has received the mighty anointing power of God, and in this place he realizes that the only thing for him to do is to submit to God. And as he submits he is more and more covered with power and led by the Spirit.

The Holy Spirit takes Jesus away into the wilderness, with its darkness and deprivation. For forty days he was without food, but because of the presence and the power of the Holy Spirit within and on him, Jesus was certain of victory. With this power he faced the wild beasts of the wilderness and the privation of every human sustenance.

And then at the end of forty days, in that holy attainment, Jesus is forced into such persecution and trial that probably has never attacked man before. And in that place God sustains him mightily. With what? With this holy—and I want you to think about it— this *holy*, blessed anointing which is upon him. This power from on high so brings prophecy to bear upon Satan that Jesus has a sword with which he can, as it were, defeat and almost slay Satan every time by reminding him, "It is written" (Luke 4:4).

In the fourteenth verse you will see the result of this wilderness victory: "Jesus returned in the power of the Spirit into Galilee: and there went out a fame of him through all the region round about. And he taught in their synagogues, being glorified of all" (vs 14-15). I want you to understand that after the trials, after all the temptations and everything, Jesus comes out more full of God, more clothed in the Spirit, more ready for the fight. The endowment with power had such an effect upon him that other people saw it and flocked to hear him, and great blessings came to the land.

Take another incident in Nazareth when Jesus is among his kinsfolk. In the spirit of this kind of holy attainment, he goes into the synagogue. There was delivered to him a book, and he read: "The Spirit of the Lord *is* upon me, because he hath anointed me to preach the gospel to the poor" (vs 18).

It is well to keep before us where the "anointing" came in. How was Jesus anointed? How did it come to him? Read again Luke's account in chapter fourteen, the first fourteen verses. Now in like manner I see that the Holy Ghost also fell upon the disciples at Pentecost. I see that they were anointed with the same power, and I see that they went forth and that success attended their ministry until the power of God swept through the inhabited world.

I want you to see that it was because of this unction, this power, that when Peter and John spoke to the lame man at the gate of the temple, he was able to rise and leap for joy. The Holy Ghost coming upon an individual is capable of changing him and fertilizing his spiritual life and filling him with such power and grace that he may not be able to foresee what would happen. What cannot happen, what is not possible, if we reach this place and if we keep in it, if we abide in it?

A PLACE OF REST

I want to turn to a portion of the Old Testament Scriptures, the thirty-seventh chapter of Ezekiel. I want you to see here particularly how a man was so full of the Spirit, was always so much in the Spirit, that he could see that the hand of the Lord was upon him. He was led out in the Spirit. He was in a place of rest, and I want you to keep that before you.

Ezekiel had come to the place where he could rest, where he knew God was with him, and that he could rest there. This is an important point. Some people have an idea that they have to be doing something by way of breaking every rule and every movement. I beseech you, by the power of the Holy Ghost today, that you see that there is one thing only that is going to accomplish the purposes of God, and that is being in the Spirit.

I don't care how dry the land is; I don't care how thirsty the land is, or how many vessels, or how few there are round about. I beseech you, in the name of Jesus, that you keep in the Spirit. That's the secret.

Ezekiel was a man who was in the right place and at the right time, and God well knew it. The Lord knows them that are his. Ezekiel said, "The Lord... carried me out in the spirit of the

Lord, and set me down in the midst of the valley, which *was* full of bones, and caused me to pass by them round about: and behold, *there were* very many in the open valley; and, lo, *they were* very dry. And he said unto me, 'Son of man, can these bones live?' And I answered, 'O Lord God, thou knowest'" (Ezekiel 37:1-3).

The vision is the Lord's, and you can see the Lord's vision only by being in the Spirit. You and I can come to a place where the dry bones and barren conditions are all around us. We might think everything is exactly opposite to our desires, and we can see no deliverance by human power. But we know that God is aware of the situation. Aware of this, we know that God wants men and women who are willing to submit, and submit, and submit, and yield, and yield, and yield to the Holy Spirit, until their bodies are saturated and soaked with God. It is then that we realize that God our Father has us in such condition that at any moment he can reveal his will to us and communicate whatever he wants to say to us.

"Can these bones live?"

"You know, O Lord."

"Yes, *I* know. What do *you* think?"

"From what I have known of you in the past, blessed Master, I believe that these dry bones can live, for you say so."

"Very true, my child. Go on and prophesy. Do as I tell you."

Now I want you to understand that there is something more in it. I want you to see that God is everything to us, and I believe that we have to come to a place where we have to submit ourselves to the mighty, anointing power of God, and where we shall see we are in the will of God. And I pray God the Holy Ghost that he will show us our leanness, our great distance from this place. What we want is a great hunger and thirst for God.

Notice what God said: "O ye dry bones, hear the word of the Lord" (vs 4). I would like you to understand that God speaks first, and he speaks so loudly and so clearly and so distinctly that this godly man (who was filled with the Spirit) heard every word. Still there was not a move in the valley. Until the word of the Lord is uttered, the bones are as dry as at the beginning.

What is the matter? God has spoken and the message has gone forth. What is it? Ah, it is only that the word of God must go forth through his servant the prophet. The world has to be brought to a knowledge of the truth, but that will only happen through human instrumentality. And that will happen when the human instrument is at a place where he will say all that the Holy Spirit directs him to say.

Ezekiel arose, and clothed with divine power, he began to speak, he began to prophesy. As soon as he began to speak, there was a rattling among the bones, and if we had been there we would have seen a bigger stir than we had ever seen before. Bone to bone at the voice of the prophet filled with the Spirit of the living God! God had given him victory.

God in like manner wants to give us victory. What does the Word say? "Be still, and know that I *am* God" (Psalm 46:10a). Be in the place of tranquility where we know that he is controlling and moving us by the mighty power of his Spirit.

Beloved, that is a place which we can reach. This prophecy is for us. Truly God wants to begin this in us. We must always remember that it is God who is the Creator, and his creative power is available at this moment. He knows where there is barrenness and where there is thirsty land, and it is he who can bring forth springs of water.

There are many dry places. Indeed, nearly every town I go to is said to be the driest of places—"the hardest town in the kingdom," they will say. How does that dryness affect you? The Lord's hand is not shortened that it cannot save. It is in humanity's extremity that God finds his opportunity, and it is for his word to awaken even you.

And so God wants us to cheer up. All things are possible to those who believe. But if we are to do the will of God at the right time and place, we must yield to the Spirit and obey him, so as to give God a fair chance.

ONLY GOD CAN MAKE THE CROOKED STRAIGHT

"So I prophesied as I was commanded," Ezekiel wrote. He just did what he was told to do. It takes more to live in that place than in any other place that I know of—to live in a place where you hear God's voice. It is only by the power of the Holy Spirit that you can do as you are told quickly and without resistance. "And as I prophesied, there was a noise, and behold, a shaking, and the bones came together, bone to his bone" (Ezekiel 37:7).

There is something worth your notice in this. It is only the Spirit who can make the crooked straight. Some of you, no doubt, have thought some of your neighbors are a bit crooked. They may be in fact some of the most crooked, off-the-way bones you have ever seen, and it would be impossible for them to get saved. That is nothing to do with you. It is for you to live in the Holy Ghost, and he can change the whole circumstance and you will be amazed at the way the crooked bones will be straightened. Nothing can change such circumstances as God can. Bone to bone, no crooked places now; but it takes God to do that.

Human beings have been trying to do it all along, but as soon as a person has been truly baptized with the Holy Ghost, God does it. There is power in the Holy Ghost to transform, renew, and change the circumstances of your life. You have to submit and let God take hold of you. Don't be troubled because you have not reached that place. You have reached somewhere, but the best is yet in store. Only yield so that he may have full control of all you are.

Let us continue this drama. What happened after the bones came together? "And when I beheld, lo, the sinews and the flesh came up upon them, and the skin covered them above: but *there was* no breath in them" (vs 8). Here is their condition: there was the form, but no breath in it. But you must never give in and think the thing is fairly accomplished if you see the joining of the members and a kind of fellowship. You must never give up with that. They are never in the royal place until the breath of God has come into them and upon them. You must always lead people to receive the Holy Ghost and know that the breath of the Almighty is upon them.

Justification will not be sufficient to accomplish the purpose of God. People may be justified and sanctified, but can never be satisfied until they are filled with the Holy Ghost. There must be a real travailing of the human heart for God to bring forth power. People are never safe until they are baptized with the Holy Ghost. That is why the apostles pressed that fact upon believers. And that is why Jesus was always pointing to the time when they should be filled with unction and power of the Spirit which would carry them all on.

Now, what did God command Ezekiel to do next? "Then said he unto me, 'Prophesy.' So I prophesied as he commanded me" (vs 9-10). Glory to God! It is most wonderful. As soon as he began to prophesy, he found there was something in it. Are you not wanting to get to that place of power? Don't you think we ought to be there? Do you think we ought to be satisfied before we are there? How can God be pleased with us until we reach that place? We must get to that place where we shall see God and know his voice, when he sends us with a message that brings life and power and victory.

When Ezekiel prophesied, an amazing thing happened to the bodies. "Breath came into them, and they lived, and stood up upon their feet, an exceedingly great army" (vs 10).

POWER EVEN IN THE BARREN PLACES

I want to point out something about John the Divine whose preaching got him into trouble. He preached all over the country, and the enemies of Christ gnashed upon him with their teeth, and they tried to the best of their power to destroy him.

Tradition says that they even put John into a pot of boiling oil, but, like a cat, he seemed to have nine lives.

I tell you there is something in the power of the Holy Spirit. When God wants to keep a man, nothing can destroy him. My life is in the hands of God. What can separate us from the love of God? Can heights or depths? Is there anything that can separate us? No, praise God! Nothing can separate us. No, John's enemies found they could not kill him, so they cast him away on the rocky and desolate island of Patmos. They thought that would be an end of him.

And there, on that lonely isle, he was "in the Spirit." Have you ever been there? The very place that was not fit for humanity was the place where John was most filled with God, and where he was most ready for the revelation of Jesus. Oh, beloved, I tell you there is something in the baptism in the Holy Ghost worthy of our whole attention, worthy of our whole consideration in every way. The baptism in the Holy Ghost! Yes, the barren wilderness, the rocky and desolate isle, the dry land, and the most unfriendly place may be filled with God.

Read the first chapter of the Revelation, and you will see that in the tenth verse John was in the Spirit on the Lord's Day, and behind him he heard "a great voice, as of a trumpet." Immediately he received a revelation, which you cannot read without being blessed. The revelation given to John contained a series of holy truths that have yet to be fulfilled, and they will be fulfilled to the letter. We read wonderful things there.

Blessed be God, we can come to that place which John speaks about. Jesus can reveal his mind to us from time to time. If you only stop to think about it, you will see you are in a position a thousand times better than John. In that barren place he was filled with the Spirit. You have no excuse, for the lines have fallen to you in pleasant places.

You will see from the second verse of the fourth chapter of Revelation that John was in such a blessed condition of fellowship with God that *immediately* he was in the Spirit. Immediately! What does that mean? It means that God wants us to be in a place where the least breath of heaven makes us all on fire, ready for everything.

You say, "How can I have that?" Oh, you can have that as easy as anything. "Can I?" Yes, it is simple as well as possible. How? Let heaven come in, let the Holy Ghost take possession of you, and when he comes into your body you will find that is the keynote of the spirit of joy and the spirit of rapture.

If you will allow the Holy Ghost to have full control, you will find you are living in the Spirit. You will discover that your opportunities will be God's opportunities. And you will find that you have come to the right place at the right time. Then the Holy Spirit will give you the exact words to speak, anointed words that will meet the need of the moment.

THE MAN AND HIS MESSAGE

From *Confidence* (Sunderland, England), June 1916, pages 102-6.

During meetings Wigglesworth conducted in Stockholm in 1921, the press and religious leaders turned on him, which led to his arrest for laying hands on the sick. Pastor Lewi Pethrus described those meetings: "His teaching was very simple and confined itself almost entirely to belief in God. Nonetheless his sermons on the promises of God were strangely convincing. He was sometimes quite drastic in his way of approaching the sick, but he won their confidence and there were many who received both mental and physical help through him. At that time we had no premise of our own.

"Wigglesworth was with us for three weeks and the meetings were mostly in the auditorium and in the YMCA. There was a general attack from the entire press, and religious leaders turned on our meetings and denounced them. What seemed to arouse most indignation was the fact that the sick were prayed for in public. This was, of course, because we had no premises of our own."[1]

NINETEEN

The Ordinary
Made Extraordinary

I love to sing that wonderful chorus, "Only Believe," because it is scriptural. It is from the words of Jesus to the ruler of the synagogue whose daughter had died (Mark 5:36):

Only believe! Only believe!
All things are possible,
Only believe!

Praise God, who has made all things possible. There is liberty for everyone, whatever the trouble. Our Lord Jesus says, "Only believe." He has obtained complete victory over every difficulty, over every power of evil, over every depravity. Every sin is covered by Calvary.

I want to talk about the tribe of Abraham. Who belongs to the tribe of Abraham? All who believe in Jesus Christ. They are the seed of faith, Abraham's seed. If we dare come believing, God will heal, God will restore, God will lift the burden and wake us up to overcoming faith.

156 / The Anointing of His Spirit

Look up! Take courage! Jesus has shaken the foundations of death and darkness. He fights for you and there is none like him. He is the great "I AM." His name is above every name. As we believe we are lifted into a place of rest, a place of conformity to God. He says to us as he did to Abraham, "I will bless you and you shall be a blessing." He says to us as he did to his people of old, "With loving kindness have I drawn you." Hallelujah!

He'll never forget to keep me,
He'll never forget to keep me;
My Father has many dear children,
But he'll never forget to keep me.

Believe it. He will never forget.

THROUGH LIPS OF CLAY

In the sixth chapter of Acts we read of the appointment of seven deacons. The disciples desired to give themselves wholly to prayer and to the ministry of the Word, so they said to the brethren, "Look ye out among you seven men of honest report, full of the Holy Ghost and wisdom, whom we may appoint over this business" (vs 3).

One of the seven was Stephen, a man "full of faith and of the Holy Ghost" (vs 5). We read that Stephen did great wonders and miracles among the people, and his opponents were not able to resist the wisdom and the Spirit by which he spoke. When his opponents brought Stephen before the Sanhedrin, all who sat in the council looked steadfastly on him, and they saw his face as if it had been the face of an angel.

I see many remarkable things in the life of Stephen. One thing moves me, and that is this truth: I must at all costs live by the power of the Spirit. God wants us to be like Stephen, full of faith and full of the Holy Ghost. You can never be the same again after you have received this wonderful baptism in the Holy Spirit.

It is important that day by day we should be full of wisdom and faith, and full of the Holy Ghost, acting by the power of the Holy Ghost. God has set us here in the last days, these days of apostasy, and would have us be burning and shining lights in the midst of an ungodly generation.

God is longing for us to come into such a fruitful position as the sons of God, with the marks of heaven upon us, his divinity bursting through our humanity, so that he can express himself through our lips of clay. God can take clay lips, weak humanity, and make an oracle for himself. He can take our frail human nature and by his divine power wash our hearts whiter than snow and make our bodies his holy temple.

Our Lord Jesus says, "All power is given unto me in heaven and in earth" (Matthew 28:18b). He longs that we should be filled with faith and with the Holy Ghost and declares to us, "He that believeth on me, the works that I do shall he do also; and greater *works* than these shall he do; because I go unto my Father" (John 14:12).

Jesus has gone to the Father. He sits in the place of power and he exercises his power not only in heaven but on earth, for he has all power on earth as well as in heaven. Hallelujah! What an open door to us if we will but believe him.

The disciples were men after the flesh just like us. God sent them forth, joined to the Lord and identified with him. Peter, John, and Thomas, how different they were! Impulsive Peter, ever ready to go forth without a stop! John, the beloved, leaning on the Master's breast, how different! Thomas, with hard nature and defiant spirit, exclaimed, "Except I shall see in his hands the print of the nails, and put my finger into the print of the nails, and thrust my hand into his side, I will not believe" (John 20:25b).

What strange flesh! How peculiar! But the Master could mold them. There was no touch like his. Under his touch even stony-hearted Thomas believed. Ah, my God, how you have had to manage some of us. Have we not been strange and very peculiar? But, oh, when God's hand comes upon us, he can speak to us in such a way—a word, a look, and we are broken.

Has he spoken to you? Thank God for his speaking. Back of all his dealings we see the love of God for us. It is not what we are that counts, but what we can be as he disciplines and chastens and transforms us by his all-skillful hands. God sees our bitter tears and our weeping night after night. There is none like him. He knows. He forgives. We cannot forgive ourselves. We oftentimes would give the world to forget, but we cannot. The devil won't let us forget. But God has forgiven and forgotten.

Do you believe self, or the devil, or God? Which are you going to believe? Believe God. I know that the past is under the blood and that God has forgiven and forgotten, for when he forgives, he forgets. Praise the Lord! Hallelujah! We are baptized to believe and to receive.

NO IFS

In making provision for the serving of tables and the daily ministering, the disciples knew who was baptized with the Holy Ghost. In the early days of the church all who took part in the work of building the kingdom had to be full of the Holy Ghost. Stephen was a man full of faith and of the Holy Ghost. God declares it. God so manifested himself in Stephen's body that this man of flesh became an epistle of truth, known and read of all. Full of faith!

I am hungry that I may be more full, that God may choose me for his service. And I know that the greatest qualification is to be filled with the Spirit. The Holy Spirit has the divine commission from heaven to impart revelation to every son of God concerning the Lord Jesus, to unfold to us the gifts and the fruit of the Spirit. He will take the things of Christ and show them to us.

Such believers never talk doubt. You never hear them say, "I wish it could be so; or if it is God's will." No *ifs*. They *know*. You never hear them say, "Well, it does not always come to pass." They say, "It is sure to be." They laugh at impossibilities and cry, "It shall be done!" Those who are full of faith hope against hope. They shout while the walls are up and the walls come down while they shout! God has this faith for us in Christ. We must be careful that no unbelief is found in us, no wavering.

"Stephen, full of faith and power, did great wonders and miracles among the people" (Acts 6:8). The Holy Ghost could do mighty things through this man because he believed God, and God is with anyone who dares to believe his Word. All things were possible because of the Holy Ghost's position in Stephen's body. He was full of the Holy Ghost so God could fulfill his purposes through him.

When a child of God is filled with the Holy Ghost, the Spirit makes intercession through him or her for the saints according to the will of God. He fills us with longings and desires until we are in a place of fervency as of a molten fire. What to do we know not.

When we are in this place the Holy Ghost begins to do. When the Holy Ghost has liberty in the body he wafts all utterance into the presence of God according to the will of God. Such prayers are always heard. Such praying is always answered; it is never bare of result. When we are praying in the Holy Ghost, faith is in evidence, and as a result, the power of God can be manifested in our midst.

When there arose certain of the various synagogues to dispute with Stephen, they were not able to resist the wisdom and the Spirit by which he spoke. When we are filled with the Holy Ghost, we will have wisdom. Praise God!

One night I was entrusted with a meeting and I was jealous of my position before God. I wanted approval from the Lord. I see that God wants sons and daughters full of the Holy Ghost, with divine ability, filled with life, a flaming fire.

In the meeting a young man stood up, a pitiful object, with a face full of sorrow. I said, "What is it, young man?" He said he was unable to work, that he could scarcely walk. He said, "I am so helpless. I have consumption and a weak heart, and my body is full of pain."

I said, "I will pray for you." And I said to the people, "As I pray for this young man, you look at his face and see it change." As I prayed his face changed and he was in a strange way. I said to him, "Go out and run a mile and come back to the meeting." He came back and said, "I can now breathe freely."

The meetings were continuing and I missed him. After a few days I saw him again in the meeting. I said, "Young man, tell the people what God has done for you." "Oh," he said, "I have been to work. I bought some papers and I have made four dollars and fifty cents." Praise God, this wonderful stream of salvation never runs dry. You can take a drink; it is close to you. It is a river that is running deep and there is plenty for all.

In another meeting a man arose and said, "Will you touch me? I am in a terrible way. I have a family of children, and through an accident in the pit I have had no work for two years. I cannot open my hands." I was full of sorrow for this poor man and something happened which had never happened before. We are in the infancy of this wonderful outpouring of the Holy Spirit and there is so much more for us. I put out my hand, and before my hands reached his, this man was loosed and made perfectly free.

I see that Stephen, full of faith and of power, did great wonders and miracles among the people. This same Holy Ghost filling is for us, and great things will be accomplished if we are filled with his Spirit. God will grant it. He declares that the desires of the righteous shall be granted. Stephen was an ordinary man made extraordinary in God.

You may be very ordinary, but God wants to make you extraordinary in the Holy Ghost. God is ready to touch and to transform you right now. Once a woman stood in a meeting asking for prayer. I prayed for her and she was healed. She cried out, "It is a miracle! It is a miracle! It is a miracle!" That is what God wants to do for us all the time. As sure as we get free in the Holy Ghost something will happen. Let us pursue the best things and let God have his right of way.

Something remarkable happened that day when Stephen stood before the council. All that sat in the council looked steadfastly on Stephen and saw his face as if it had been the face of an angel. It was worth being filled with the Holy Ghost for that. The Spirit breaking through. There is a touch of the Spirit where the light of God will verily radiate from our faces.

A RADIANT DEATH

The seventh chapter of Acts records the profound, prophetic utterance that the Spirit spoke through this holy man. The word of God flowed through the lips of Stephen in the form of divine prophecy so that those who heard these things were cut to the heart. "But he, being full of the Holy Ghost, looked up steadfastly into heaven, and saw the glory of God, and Jesus standing on the right hand of God, and said, 'Behold, I see the heavens opened, and the Son of man standing on the right hand of God'" (vs 55-56).

Right to the last Stephen was full of the Holy Ghost. He saw Jesus standing. In another part we read of Christ seated at the right hand of God. That is his place of authority. But here we see that he arose. Jesus was so keenly interested in that martyr, Stephen, that he stood up. May the Lord open our eyes to see him and to know that he is deeply interested in all that concerns us. He is touched with the feeling of our infirmities.

All things are naked and open to the eyes of our God. That asthma, he knows. That rheumatism, he knows. That pain in the back, that head, those feet, he knows. God wants to loose every captive and to set you free just as he has set me free. I do not know that I have a body today. I am free of every human ailment, absolutely free.[1] Christ has redeemed us. He has power over all the power of the enemy and has wrought a great victory. Will you have it? It is yours—a perfect redemption.

And they stoned Stephen, who called upon God and said, "'Lord Jesus, receive my spirit.' And he kneeled down, and cried with a loud voice, 'Lord, lay not this sin to their charge.' And when he had said this, he fell asleep" (Acts 7:59-60). Stephen was not only filled with faith, but he was also filled with love as he prayed just as his Master had prayed, "Father, forgive them" (Luke 23:34a).

It is God's intention to make us a new creation, with all the old things passed away and all things within us truly of God, to bring in a new, divine order, a perfect love, and an unlimited faith. Will you have it? Redemption is free. Arise in the activity of faith and God will heal you as you rise. Only believe and receive in faith. Stephen, full of faith and of the Holy Ghost, did great signs and wonders. May God bless to us this word and fill us full of his Holy Spirit, and through the power of the Holy Ghost more and more reveal Christ in us.

The Spirit of God will always reveal the Lord Jesus Christ. Serve him, love him, be filled with him. It is lovely to hear him as he makes himself known to us. Jesus is the same yesterday, today, and forever. He is willing to fill us with the Holy Ghost and faith, just as he filled Stephen.

THE MAN AND HIS MESSAGE

Originally titled "Full! Full! Full!" from the *Pentecostal Evangel* (Springfield, Missouri), June 12, 1926, pages 2-3.

When the pentecostal movement began at the turn of the twentieth century, existing denominations rejected the experience of the baptism in the Holy Spirit with the evidence of speaking in tongues (Acts 2:4). Critics labeled it as heresy or worse.

Smith Wigglesworth belonged to the criticized crowd, but he refused to compromise his pentecostal beliefs.

Michael Harper, an Anglican priest involved in the charismatic renewal, wrote of a nonpentecostal meeting which Wigglesworth attended. "None of the speakers seemed to get to the point. So Wigglesworth, taking his jacket off, strode to the front and fired off some good pentecostal broadsides. Although we can admire his courage, his method was not likely to commend itself to the intractable antagonists of the pentecostal experience. But we must understand the feelings of men who suffered the most terrible reproach and ridicule from their Christian brethren."[2]

TWENTY

Showing Forth the Glory of God

These are the last days, the days of the falling away. These are days when Satan is having a great deal of power. But we must keep in mind that Satan has power only as he is allowed. It is a great thing to know that God is loosing you from the world, loosing you from a thousand things. You must seek to have the mind of God in all things. If you don't, you will stop his working.

I had to learn that lesson as I was on a ship en route to Australia. We stopped at a place called Aden, where they were selling all kinds of wares. Among other things were some beautiful rugs and ostrich feathers in great quantities. There was a gentleman in the first-class section of the ship who wanted feathers. He bought one lot, but the next lot for sale was too big; he didn't want so many. He said to me, "Will you join me?" I knew *I* didn't want feathers for I had no room or use for them and wouldn't know what to do with them if I got them.

However, this man pleaded with me to join him. I perceived it was the Spirit as clearly as anything, so I said yes. We agreed to buy the feathers for the sum of fifteen dollars. Then I found the man had no money on him, but said he had plenty in his cabin. I perceived it was the Spirit again, so it fell to my lot to pay for the feathers. The man said to me, "I will get the money and give it to one of the stewards." I replied, "No, that's not the way to do business. I'm known all over the ship. You seek me out."

When the man brought the money to me, I said to him, "God wants me to talk to you. Now sit down." So he sat down and in ten minutes the whole of his life was unhinged, unraveled, and broken up—so broken that like a big baby he wept and cried for salvation. It was the feathers that did it.

But you know we shall never know the *mind* of God till we learn to know the *voice* of God. The striking thing about Moses is that it took him forty years to learn human wisdom, forty years to know his helplessness, and forty years to live in the power of God. One hundred and twenty years it took to teach that man—and sometimes it seems to me it will take many years to bring us just where we can recognize the voice of God, the leadings of God, and all his will concerning us.

I see that all revelation, all illumination, everything that God had in Christ was to be brought forth into perfect light that we might be able to live the same, produce the same, and be in every activity sons of God with power. We must not limit the Holy One. And we must clearly see that God brought us forth to make us supernatural; that we might be changed all the time on the line of the supernatural; that we may every day live so in the Spirit, that all of the revelations of God are just like a canvas thrown before our eyes, on which we see clearly step by step all the divine will of God.

WE MUST BE AS SIMPLE AS BABIES

Any assembly that puts its hand upon the working of the Spirit will surely dry up. The assembly must be as free in the Spirit as possible. Unless we are very wise, we can easily quench the power of God which is upon us. It is an evident fact that one person in a meeting, filled with unbelief, can make a place for the devil to have a seat. And it is very true that if we are not careful we may quench the spirit of some person who is innocent but incapable of helping himself. "We then that are strong ought to bear the infirmities of the weak" (Romans 15:1).

If you want an assembly full of life, you must have one in which the Spirit of God is manifested. And to keep at the boiling pitch of that blessed incarnation of the Spirit, you must be as simple as babies; you must be as harmless as doves and as wise as serpents.

I always ask God for a leading of grace. It takes grace to be in a meeting, because it is so easy if you are not careful to get on the natural side. The man who is a preacher, if he has lost the anointing, will be well repaid if he will repent and get right with God and get the unction back. It never pays us to be less than spiritual, and we must have a divine language, and the language must be of God.

Beloved, if you come into perfect line with the grace of God, one thing will certainly take place in your life. You will change from that old position of the world's line—where you were judging everybody and where you were not trusting anyone—and come into a place where you will have a heart that will believe all things, a heart that under no circumstances reviles again when you are reviled.

I know many of you think many times before you speak once. Here is a great word: "For your obedience is come abroad unto all *men*. I am glad therefore on your behalf: but yet I would have you wise unto that which is good, and simple concerning evil" (Romans 16:19). Innocent. No inward corruption or defilement that is full of distrusts, but just a holy, divine likeness of Jesus that dares believe that God Almighty will surely watch over all. Hallelujah!

"There shall no evil befall thee, neither shall any plague come nigh thy dwelling. For he shall give his angels charge over thee, to keep thee in all thy ways" (Psalm 91:10-11). The child of God who is rocked in the bosom of the Father has the sweetest touch of heaven. If the saints only knew how precious they are in the sight of God, they would scarcely be able to sleep for thinking of his watchful, loving care.

Oh, he is a precious Jesus! He is a lovely Savior! He is divine in all his attitude toward us and makes our hearts burn. There is nothing like it. "Oh," they said on the road to Emmaus, "did not our heart burn within us, while as he talked with us by the way?" (Luke 24:32). Oh, beloved, it must be so today.

ON FIRE FOR GOD

Always keep in your mind the fact that the Holy Ghost must bring manifestations. We must understand that the Holy Ghost is breath, the Holy Ghost is person, and it is the most marvelous thing to me to know that this Holy Ghost power can be in every part of your body. You can feel it from the crown of your head to the soles of your feet. Oh, it is lovely to be burning all over with the Holy Ghost!

And when that takes place there is nothing but the operation of the tongue that must give forth the glory and the praise. You must be in the place of magnifying the Lord. The Holy Ghost is the great magnifier of Jesus, the great illuminator of Jesus. And so after the Holy Ghost comes in it is impossible to keep your tongue still. Why, you would burst if you didn't give him utterance. Talk about a dumb [silent] baptized soul? Such a person is not to be found in the Scriptures.

You will find that when you speak to God in the new tongue he gives you, you enter into a close communion with him hitherto unexperienced. Talk about preaching! I would like to know how it will be possible for all the people filled with the Holy Ghost to stop preaching. Even the sons and daughters must prophesy. After the Holy Ghost comes in, a person is in a new order in God. You will find it so real that you will want to sing, talk, laugh, and shout. We are in a strange place when the Holy Ghost comes in.

If the *incoming* of the Spirit is lovely, what must be the *outflow?* The purpose of the incoming is only to be an outflow. I am very interested in the scenery wherever I travel. When I was in Switzerland I wouldn't be satisfied till I went to the top of the mountain, though I like the valleys as well. On the summit of the mountain the sun beats on the snow and sends the water trickling down the mountains right through to the meadows. Go there and see if you can stop it.

Just so in the spiritual. God begins with the divine flow of his eternal power which is the Holy Ghost, and you cannot stop it. We must always clearly see that the baptism with the Spirit must make us ministering spirits. Peter and John had been baptized only a short time. Did they know what they had? No. I defy you to know what you have. No one knows what you have in the baptism with the Holy Ghost. You have no conception of it. You cannot measure it by any human standards. No one has any idea how great is the baptism with the Holy Spirit.

Likewise, Peter and John had no idea what they had. For the first time after they were baptized in the Holy Ghost, they came down to the Gate Beautiful. There they saw a man who for forty years had been lame. What was the first thing they did after they saw him sitting there? *Ministration.* What was the second? *Operation.* What was the third? *Manifestation,* of course. It could not be otherwise. You will always find that this order in the Scripture will be carried out in everybody.

I clearly see that we ought to have spiritual giants in the earth, mighty in understanding, amazing in activity, always having a wonderful report because of their activity in faith. I find instead that there are many people who perhaps have better discernment than you, better knowledge of the Word than you, but they have failed to put it into practice, so these gifts lie dormant.

I am here to help you to begin on the sea of life with mighty acts in the power of God through the gifts of the Spirit. You will find that this on which I am speaking is out of knowledge derived from a wonderful experience in many lands. The man who is filled with the Holy Ghost is always acting. Look for our best example in the first verse of the Acts of the Apostles: "Jesus began both to do and teach." He began to do first, and so must we.

MINISTRATION, OPERATION, MANIFESTATION

Beloved, we must see that the baptism with the Holy Ghost is an activity with an outward manifestation. When I was in Norway, God was mightily moving there, even though I had to talk through an interpreter. However, God always worked in a wonderful way. One day while four of us were walking down the street, a man stopped and wanted to talk with us. I looked back and saw that the man was in a dilemma, so I returned to where they were standing and asked the interpreter, "What is the trouble?"

"This man," he said, "is so full of neuralgia that he is almost blind, and he is in a terrible state." As soon as they finished the conversation, I said to the spirit that was afflicting him, "Come out of him in the name of Jesus." And the man cried, "It is all gone! It is all gone! I am free." Brothers and sisters, we have no conception of what God has for us!

In Sydney, Australia, a man with a walking stick passed my friend and me. He had to get down and then twist over, and the tortures of his face made a deep impression on my soul. I asked myself, *Is it right to pass this man?* So I said to my friend, "There is a man in awful distress, and I cannot go farther. I must speak to him."

Going to the man I said, "You seem to be in great trouble." "Yes," he answered, "I am no good and never will be." I said to him, "You see that hotel [which was where I was staying]. Be in front of that door in five minutes and I will pray for you, and you shall be as straight as any man in this place." This is on the line of activity in the faith of Jesus. I came back after paying a bill, and he was there. I will never forget him wondering if he was going to be trapped, or what was up that a man should stop him in the street and tell him he should be made straight. I had said it, so it must be.

If you say anything, you must stand with God to make it so. Never say anything for bravado without having the right to say it. Always be sure of your ground and that you are honoring God. If there is anything about it to bring you personal gain, it will bring you sorrow. Your whole ministry will have to be on the line of grace and blessing.

We helped the crippled man up the two steps, helped him to the elevator, and took him upstairs. It seemed difficult to get him from the elevator to my room, as though Satan was making the last stroke for his life, but we got him there. Then in five minutes' time this man walked out of that bedroom as straight as any man in this place. He walked perfectly and declared he hadn't a pain in his body.

Oh, brothers and sisters, it is *ministration*, it is *operation*, it is *manifestation!* Those are three of the leading principles of the baptism with the Holy Ghost. And we must see to it that God is producing these three through us. The Bible is the Word of God. It has the truths, and whatever people may say of them, they stand stationary, unmovable. Not one jot or tittle shall fail of all his good promises. His Word will come forth. In heaven it is settled; on earth it must be made manifest that he is the God of everlasting power.

God wants manifestation and he wants his glory to be seen. He wants us all to be filled with that line of thought so that he can look upon us and delight in us, subduing the world unto him. And so you are going to miss a great deal if you don't begin to act. But once you begin to act in the order of God, you will find that God establishes your faith and from that day starts you on the line of the promises.

When will you begin? Beloved, we will have no idea what God has for us until we will only begin! But, oh, the grace we need! We may make a mishap. If we do it outside of him, if we do it for ourselves, and if we want to be someone, it will be a failure. We shall only be able to do well as we do it in the name of Jesus.

Oh, the love that God's Son can put into us if we are only humble enough, weak enough, and helpless enough to know that except he does it, it will not be done! "What things soever you desire, when you pray, believe that you receive them, and you shall have them." Live in the Spirit, walk in the Spirit, walk in the communion of the Spirit, talk with God. All leadings of the divine order are for you. I pray that if you have turned to your own way and have made God second, you will come to repentance on all lines. Separate yourself from every material desire, and God will use you for his glory. Begin with God this moment.

THE MAN AND HIS MESSAGE

Originally titled "The Active Life of the Spirit-Filled Believer" from *The Elim Evangel* (London, England), March 31, 1947, pages 161-63. This sermon was published with the news that Smith Wigglesworth had died on March 12 while attending the funeral of an old friend. Following his death, Mrs. Freida Birney of Sunderland, England, wrote to Stanley H. Frodsham about a 1932 missionary convention at which Wigglesworth presided: "He announced at one of the meetings that he had asked the Lord for another fifteen years of life. It is remarkable that it was fifteen years to the very week that the Lord took him home."[1]

TWENTY-ONE

God's Treasure House

How exhaustless is the treasure house of the Most High! How near God is to us when we are willing to draw nigh! And how he comes with refreshing to us when our hearts are attuned and desiring him only, for the desires of the righteous shall be granted.

God has for us today a stimulation of divine acquaintance, a life divine to flow through our being that shall be sufficient for us in all times of need. When God is for us, who can be against us? What a blessed assurance this is to the hungry heart. How it thrills one to the very depths of the soul.

My heart's desire is that I bring you again to a banquet, that wonderful reserve, that great blessed day of appointment for us with the King, that we may believe that all the precious promises are "yea" and "amen" to us as we dare to believe.

Oh, to believe God! Oh, to rest upon what he says, for there is not one jot or tittle of the Word which shall fail till all is fulfilled! Has he not promised and will he not also perform? Our blessed Lord of life and glory impressed upon us before he left that he would send the Comforter, who would take the words of Jesus and would pray through us, and whatsoever he would ask, the Lord would hear us. So I want you to get in a definite place, daring to ask God for something that shall be the means of stimulating your life forever.

Are you ready? You ask, "What for?" To have some of God's promises fulfilled. Are you ready? What for? That God shall this day so clothe you with the Spirit that there shall be nothing within that shall war against the Spirit. Are you ready? Search your heart diligently. Are you ready? What for? That you may know the Word of God, that those who dwell and live in the Spirit of God are kept in perfect condition of no condemnation.

I am so desirous that you should get so stimulated with this prospective condition, then come into a realizing condition, because that is what God wants you to have, to get so moved by the power of God to believe that the things that you hear shall be yours. So many people miss a great many things because they are always thinking it was for someone else. I want you to know that God's Word is for *you* and you are to make a personal application of all there is in the Scriptures.

I do not believe the Scriptures are only for pastors, teachers, evangelists, prophets, apostles. Rather, they are for the whole body of Christ, for it is the body that has to be the epistle of Christ. So the Word of God has to abound in you till you are absolutely built and fixed upon the living Word.

BE NOT IGNORANT

I am going to read again the fourteenth chapter of 1 Corinthians, the twelfth verse, because I want to make it the keynote of all that is spoken today: "Even so ye, forasmuch as you are zealous of spiritual *gifts*, seek that ye may excel to the edifying of the church." Keep that definitely before your mind, because whatever happens in a service means nothing to me unless it leads to edification or comfort or consolation.

God wants to make you worthy of his wonderful name. Only you must always understand that all the gifts and graces of the Spirit are most helpful to you as you are a blessing to others. The Holy Ghost came not to exalt you, but that you should exalt the Lord.

Before these services are over I shall be able to tell you definitely how to receive a gift, then how to use a gift, or how to be in a place where the gift can be used. We should cover much ground because the Spirit is going to speak. If I use my own reasoning, you won't be edified. There is only one edification that is going to last, and it is the spiritual, inward revelation of Christ.

Brain matter is no good without it being spiritually quickened through the heart affections. So let us remember it is more important that we should be filled with the Holy Ghost, that the Spirit should have its perfect control and way, than that we should be filled with knowledge to no profit. Knowledge puffs up; a little knowledge is dangerous. In fact, all knowledge is in very great danger unless it is balanced in a perfect place where God has the controlling position.

Reviewing the first few verses of the twelfth chapter of 1 Corinthians, we find the Holy Ghost is speaking. He would not have you ignorant concerning spiritual gifts, he says. You are not to be ignorant of the best gift God has arranged for you. You are to come into possession of it. This gift is an inheritance that has been left by God's Son. He rose to carry it out, and he is on the throne to carry out his own will. His will is that you should be filled with all the fulness of God. Wonderful will!

The next thought is that God has entrusted to the Gentiles the proclamation of the gospel in the power and demonstration of the Spirit, that we may not speak with human wisdom, but by the oracles of the operation of God. So the Holy Ghost is to make us ready for every perfect work, and so ready that we take advantage of every opportunity. Just as much as if Jesus were in the world, we must be in the world: ready for the glorious, blessed anointing and equipping for service, that the powers of hell shall not prevail, but that we may bind the powers of Satan.

Tongues with interpretation: "The Spirit himself brings forth light and truth to edify and build up the church in the most holy faith, that we might be ready for all activity in God. For the Spirit of the Lord is upon us to bring forth that which God has declared and ordained, that we should go forth bearing precious fruit, and come forth rejoicing, singing, and harvesting together.

"Oh, to keep in the covenant place where you are hidden in Christ, where he alone is superseding, controlling, leading, directing, and causing you to live only for the glory of God!"

CHANGED FROM GLORY TO GLORY

We pass on to the third verse of 1 Corinthians 12: "No man speaking by the Spirit of God calleth Jesus accursed." Don't forget that you are entrusted with the Word of life, which speaks to you as the truth. Jesus is the way, the truth, and the life, and he declared eternal life by the operation of the gospel; for we receive immortality and life by the gospel. Seeing these things are so, you can understand that those who receive the life of Christ pass out of condemnation into eternal life.

But what about those who do not? They are still under condemnation, without hope and without God in the world, and in danger of eternal destruction. God save them! Hellfire will never be changed by what people say about it. Hellfire will be the same forever. You will never change the Word of God by human opinions. The Word of God is fixed forever.

The Lord wants you to be in a great place, with the Holy Ghost having such control of your inner eyes to reveal the fulness of the Lord of Life, till Jesus is magnified tremendously by the revelation of the Holy Ghost, till he becomes Lord over all things—over your affections, your will, your purposes, your plans, and your wishes forever. Let him be Lord.

Tongues with interpretation: "For when the Lord changes the situation, then you come out of the hiding of captivity into the fulness of the revelation of the blaze of his glory. For when he has molded you, then he can build you and change you till he is having his way."

It is a great purpose that God has for us, that we can be changed, and you are in a great place when you are willing to have this change take place. You are in a greater place when you are willing to drop everything that has brought you to where you thought you could not be changed. And when you have dropped all things that have hindered you, you have leaped forth and been tremendously changed.

If you have held anything on a human plane, no matter how it has come, if it is not according to the biblical standard, let it be weeded out. If you do not get it weeded out, there is a time coming that wood, hay, and stubble will be burned, while the gold, silver, and precious stones will stand the fire.

Many people would like to know what kind of crown they will have when they get to glory. Well, the Lord will take everything that could not be burnt by the fire and make your own crown. So everybody is forming his or her own crown. Now you be careful not to be all wood, hay, and stubble. Have something left for the crown. There is a crown of life that fades not away that I am trying to help you to build for today.

BE ON GUARD AGAINST THE "BUTS"

God has a particularizing way of meeting particular people of today. Each of us is different—in our faces, in our makeup—so God has a way to particularize a gift that would fit you perfectly so that you will not be lopsided. I am trusting the Lord to help me to build you without being unbalanced.

Many people have good things—*but*. Many people might be remarkably used—*but*. Many people might soar into wonderful places of divine positions with God—*but*. And it is the *"but"* that spoils it. Some people have a very good gift—all the gifts of God are good—but because the gift has been made a blessing, they transgress with the same gift and speak in tongues longer than they ought to. So it is the "but" in the way that is spoiling the best.

Some people have wonderful prophecy, but there is a "but." They have prophesied and the Lord has used them in the prophecy, but because others have applauded them in that gift, they have gone beyond divine prophecy and used their own human mind. The "but" has spoiled them till they do not want the hidden prophecy. Sister so-and-so has a wonderful testimony and we all like to hear her for three minutes, but we are all sick of it if she goes on five minutes. Why so? There is a "but" about it. Brother so-and-so kindles fire in every prayer meeting when he begins to speak, but after about five minutes all the people say, "I wish he would stop." There is a "but" there.

Because of this human tendency to become lopsided, I want to speak advisedly that you do not transgress. Do not use divine liberty to spoil God's position, but be wise and the Lord will make you understand what it means. Be wise.

When you say that you have been baptized with the Holy Ghost, people look and say, "Well, if that be so, there ought to be something very beautiful." Yes, it is true, and if there is something which is shady or uncanny, not expressing the glory or grace, the meekness or the love of Christ, there is a "but" about it. The "but" is that you have not really got your own human spirit under control by the divine Spirit. The mingling of the human is spoiling the divine.

Now, a word for the wise is sufficient, and if you are not wise after you have heard, it shows that you are foolish. Do not be foolish: be wise! Let not your goodness be spoken of as evil. God wants a people in these days who are so fortified, so built in Christ, that they need not be ashamed.

Tongues with interpretation: "*For it is God who has called you for his own purpose. It is Christ who ordained you, and being ordained by Christ, we go forth to bring forth much fruit. And God is being glorified when our anointing or our covenant with Christ is reserved for God only, and we live and move for the glory of the exhibition of Christ. That is the place where Jesus is highly honored; and when you pray, God is glorified in the Son; and when you preach, the unction abides, and the Lord brings forth blessing upon the hearers.*"

TAKEN CAPTIVE BY CHRIST

In the fourth to seventh verses of the twelfth chapter of 1 Corinthians you notice very remarkable words. In this passage we are dealing with the Spirit, with the Lord Jesus, and with God, every one of them in cooperation with this position. Let us read those verses: "Now there are diversities of gifts, but the same Spirit. And there are differences of administrations, but the same Lord. And there are diversities of operations, but it is the same God which worketh all in all. But the manifestation of the Spirit is given to every man to profit withal."

There are diversities, varieties of gifts which truly are to be in the believer. First Corinthians goes on to list nine gifts of the Holy Ghost, but I would like you to notice that they never interfere with the gifts that Jesus bestows. If you turn to Ephesians 4 you will find that Jesus has gifts which aren't included in the twelfth chapter of 1 Corinthians. Let us look at the gifts of Jesus, how beautifully God arranges the thing. "When he ascended up on high, he led captivity captive, and gave gifts unto men" (Ephesians 4:8).

Paul was in captivity. How do we know? Because Paul describes his position as the chief of sinners. And as long as we know the *chief* of sinners has been saved, then we know that every person who ever lives can be saved. This chief of sinners was led captive when he was filled with indignation against the disciples, when he was rushing everywhere to apprehend them and put them in prison and make them blaspheme that same name.

Paul was held in the captivity of Satan. Jesus took him out of that captivity and brought him into his captivity, and gave him gifts. Jesus has already made disciples and has gone up on high leading captivity captive; then he is giving gifts. "And he gave some, apostles; and some, prophets; and some, evangelists; and some, pastors and teachers; For the perfecting of the saints, for the work of the ministry, for the edifying of the body of Christ" (Ephesians 4:11-12). This is the divine position of our Lord, giving gifts to those he has in captivity.

Now who do you think is most likely to be held in captivity in this meeting? The people who are lost in God, hidden. Being baptized in water is an emblem of death, and the moment a person is immersed in the water, he or she is lifted out. But not so with the baptism with the Holy Spirit. To be baptized in the Holy Ghost is every day to be deeper in, never lifted out, never coming out—held in captivity and ready for gifts.

WHO HAS A RIGHT TO THE EPISTLES?

Now, is a person made a prophet or an apostle or a teacher before the baptism of the Spirit or after? I want to speak to you very definitely, and I want you to keep in mind what the Spirit shall say to us at this time. When I went to New Zealand, the power of God was very present, and he wonderfully worked miracles and wonders there. And the gift that laid hold of the whole place was the gift of tongues and interpretation. It moved the whole of that city till the place which held thirty-five hundred people often was overcrowded, and we had two and three thousand more who could not get in.

Now when the Plymouth Brethren, who knew the Word of God, saw the grace of God upon me, they wanted to talk with me. So I scheduled a time and eighteen of them came. They began by saying, "Well, we know God is with you; it is clearly proven." (In ten days we had two thousand people saved, and fifteen hundred of those young converts sat down to breaking bread. And it was the Plymouth Brethren who served us the wine and the bread.)

"Now," they went on, "we want to examine the truth with you to see where things stand." I said, "All right, brethren." In a moment or two they were quoting to me from Ephesians. "But," I said, "beloved, you know better than anybody that the person that climbs up some other way is a thief and a robber, don't you? How many times have you preached that? Jesus is the door, and everyone entering that way shall be saved. What does it mean? Jesus is truth."

They continued quoting to me from Ephesians. "But, brethren," said I, "you have no right to Ephesians; you have no right to the epistles. The epistles are not for you. You are climbing up some other way." Without fear of contradiction, on the authority of God, I say today, there is no person in this place who has a right to the epistles until they have gone through the Acts of the Apostles and received the Holy Ghost.

The Plymouth Brethren said I could not prove it. I said, "I can prove it very easily." And I read, "For he that speaketh in an *unknown* tongue speaketh not unto men, but unto God: for no man understands *him*, howbeit in the spirit he speaketh mysteries" (1 Corinthians 14:2).

"Now, brethren, tell me if you understand that." They answered no. "Simply because you have never received the Holy Ghost. Every person who receives the Holy Ghost receives that gift, speaking unto God by the Spirit. The Gospels are the gospel of the kingdom. The Acts of the Apostles are where people see water baptism, sanctification, and also see the fulfilled receiving of the Holy Ghost. So the moment you pass through the Acts of the Apostles you are ready for the epistles, for the epistles are written to baptized believers.

"I will prove it another way," I said, and read Romans 8: 26-27: "Likewise the Spirit also helpeth our infirmities: for we know not what we should pray for as we ought: but the Spirit itself maketh intercession for us with groanings which cannot be uttered. And he that searcheth the hearts knoweth what *is* the mind of the Spirit, because he maketh intercession for the saints according to *the will of* God." Here is another distinct position of a person filled with the Holy Ghost. That is not the Spirit of Christ; that is the Holy Spirit. There is quite a difference between the Spirit of Christ and the Holy Spirit.[1]

Tongues with interpretation: "For the Lord himself is the chief director of all truth, for he is the way and the truth. Therefore the Spirit takes the Word, which is Christ, and reveals it unto us, for he is the life by the Word. 'He who hears my word and believes on him that sent me has everlasting life.' Jesus is the way, Jesus is the truth, Jesus is the life."

BEATITUDES OF THE SPIRIT

The Holy Spirit burns with a godly jealousy over you. Why? Lest you should turn to yourself. He wants you entirely to exhibit the Lord, so he girds you, sees to you in every way, that you will not be drawn aside by human desires, but that Jesus shall become the alpha and omega in all your desires.

Now to this end the Spirit knows the great hunger of the heart. What for? Gifts, graces, beatitudes. Oh, it is lovely when we can pray only in the Holy Ghost! I am going to give you a very important word about the value of praying in the Spirit. Lots of people are still without an understanding as to what it is to pray in the Spirit. In 1 Corinthians 14:15 we read: "I will pray with the spirit, and I will pray with the understanding also: I will sing with the spirit, and I will sing with the understanding also."

Tongues with interpretation: "It is only he, it is he who rolls away the cloud. He alone is the one who lifts the fallen, cheers the faint, brings fresh oil, and changes the countenance. It is the Lord your God. He has seen your misery; he has known your heartbrokenness; and he has known how near you seem to despair...."

Oh, beloved, God is in the midst of us to help us into these wonderful, divine places of appointment! Are you ready? You ask, "What for?" To let all differences cease and to have the same evidence they had in the upper room. Are you ready? What for? To be in the place for God's Son to be pleased, where he gives you all the desires of your heart. Are you ready? What for? That God can fill you with new life, stimulate you with new fire, inflame you with great desire.

We are in the midst of blessing; I want you to be blessed. Faith is the greatest positioner that brings us evidence. Faith is that which will lift you into every place, if you do not interfere with it. Don't forget that you are in the presence of God. This day has to be covered with a greater day. It is not what you are; it is what you are intending to be. If you have spoken in tongues, believe it is your right and your privilege to have anything in the Bible. Don't let your human mind interfere with the great plan of God. Submit yourself to God.

May the divine likeness of him who is the express image of the Father dwell in you richly, abounding through all, supplying every need, bringing you into a place where you know the hand of God is leading you from treasure to treasure, from grace to grace, from victory to victory, from glory unto glory, by the Spirit of the Lord.

THE MAN AND HIS MESSAGE

From *Bridal Call Foursquare* (Los Angeles, California), August 1927, pages 21-23, 31-32. Preached at Aimee Semple McPherson's Angelus Temple.

Wigglesworth had been a pentecostal for twenty years when he preached this message. Back in 1907, his baptism in the Holy Spirit shocked more than a few people in Bradford, including his

continued on page 184

wife. After he delivered a sermon from Luke 4:18-19, an impressed Polly—the preacher in the family—knew "her Smith" was a different man than he had been before going to Sunderland.

"That night she witnessed the beginning of a ministry which was to take her husband around the world. She was not by any means the only person to notice the difference, for when Wigglesworth had finished speaking and sat down, the secretary of the mission sprang to his feet and said, 'I want what our leader has received.'"[2] Polly too was baptized in the Spirit and was a dynamic preacher until her untimely death in 1913.

TWENTY-TWO

Aflame for God

C hrist said to his disciples just before he ascended, "Ye shall receive power, after the Holy Ghost is come upon you: and ye shall be witnesses unto me" (Acts 1:8a). On the day of Pentecost, he sent the power as promised. And the remainder of the Acts of the Apostles tells of the witnessing of these Spirit-filled disciples, the Lord working with them and confirming the word with signs following.

The Lord Jesus is just the same today. The anointing is just the same. The pentecostal experience is just the same. And we are to look for like results as set forth in Luke's record of what happened in the days of the early church.

John the Baptist said concerning Jesus, "He shall baptize you with the Holy Ghost, and *with* fire" (Matthew 3:11b). God's ministers are to be a flame of fire—a perpetual flame, a constant fire, a continual burning, shining lights. God has nothing less for us than to be flames. We must have a living faith in God, a belief that his great might and power may flame through us until our whole lives are energized by his power.

When the Holy Ghost comes he comes to enable us to show forth Jesus Christ in all his glory, to make him known as the one who heals today as in the days of old. The baptism in the Spirit enables us to preach as they did at the beginning, through the power of the Holy Ghost sent down from heaven and with the manifestation of the gifts of the Spirit. Oh, if we would only let the Lord work in us, melting us until a new mandate arises, moved with his compassion!

God was wonderfully with me as I traveled by ship from Egypt to Italy. Every hour I was conscious of his blessed presence. When a man on board suddenly collapsed, his wife was terribly alarmed, along with everybody else. Some said that he was about to expire. But I saw it was just a glorious opportunity for the power of God to be manifested.

Oh, what it means to be a flame of fire, to be indwelt by the living Christ! We are behind time if we have to pray for power when an occasion like that comes, or if we have to wait until we feel a sense of his presence. The Lord's promise was, "You shall receive power after the Holy Ghost is come upon you." And if we will believe, the power of God will be always manifested when there is a definite need. When you exercise your faith, you will find you have a greater power than that in the world. Oh, to be awakened out of unbelief into a place of daring for God on the authority of his blessed Book!

So right there on board that ship, in the name of Jesus, I rebuked the devil. To the astonishment of the man's wife and the man himself, he was able to stand. He said, "What is this? It is going all over me. I have never felt anything like this before." From the top of his head to the soles of his feet the power of God shook him. God has given us authority over all the power of the devil. Oh, that we may live in the place where we realize this always!

MORE THAN CONQUERORS

Christ, who is the express image of God, has come to our human weaknesses, to change them and us into divine likeness, to make us partakers of the divine nature, so that by the power of his might we may not only overcome but also rejoice in the fact that we are more than conquerors.

God wants you to know by experience what it means to be more than a conqueror. The baptism in the Holy Spirit has come for nothing less than to empower you, to give you the very power that Christ himself had, so that you, a yielded vessel, may continue the same type of ministry that Jesus had when he walked this earth in the days of his flesh. He purposes that you should come behind in no gift. There are gifts of healing and the working of miracles, but they must be apprehended. There is the gift of faith by the same Spirit which you are to receive.

The need in the world today is that we should be burning and shining lights to reflect the glory of Christ. We cannot do this with a cold, indifferent experience, and we never shall. His servants are to be flames of fire. Christ came that we might have life, and life more abundantly. And we are to give that life to others, to be ministers of the life and power and healing virtue of Jesus Christ wherever we go.

Some years ago I was in Ceylon [Sri Lanka]. In one place my fellow workers complained, "Four days is not much to give us." "No," I said "but it is a good share." They said to me, "We are not touching the people here at all." I asked, "Can you have a meeting early in the morning, at eight o'clock?" They said they would. So I instructed them, "Tell all the mothers who want their babies to be healed to come, and all the people over seventy to come, and after that we hope to give an address to the people to make them ready for the baptism in the Spirit." It would have done you good to see the four hundred mothers coming at eight o'clock with their babies, and then to see the 150 old people with their white hair coming to be healed.

We need to have something more than smoke to touch the people; we need to be a burning fire for God. His ministers must be flames of fire. In those days in Ceylon thousands came out to hear the Word of God. I believe there were about three thousand people crying for mercy at once. It was a great sight. From that first morning the meetings grew to such an extent that I would estimate every time some five to six thousand gathered, while I had to preach in a temperature of 110 degrees.

Then I had to pray for these people who were sick. But I can tell you, a flame of fire can do anything. Things change in the fire.

This was Pentecost in our midst. But here's what moved me more than anything else: there were hundreds who tried to touch me, they were so impressed with the power of God that was present. And many testified that with that touch they were healed. It was not that there was any virtue in me. The people's faith was exercised as it was in Jerusalem when they believed Peter's shadow would heal them.

You can receive something in three minutes that you can carry with you into glory. What do you want? Is anything too hard for God? God can meet you now. God sees inwardly; he knows all about you. Nothing is hidden from him. And he can satisfy the soul and give you a spring of eternal blessing that will carry you right through.

THE MAN AND HIS MESSAGE

From the *Pentecostal Evangel* (Springfield, Missouri), October 17, 1942, page 5.

While conducting a meeting in Switzerland, Wigglesworth and the sponsoring pastor were told that a blind man had come to the mission, saying he would not leave until he received new eyes. Wigglesworth turned to the pastor and said, "Brother Ruft, this is the opportunity of our lives." They hurried back to the mission and prayed for the determined man. He was healed instantly and rushed home to see his father and mother. That night when Wigglesworth and the pastor arrived at the meeting place, the man who had been blind was telling his story. Wigglesworth wrote, "I did not preach that night, for the blind man completely took the meeting out of my hands. We surely had a wonderful time, for God gave us a great visitation."[1]

PART FOUR:

Yielding to the Holy Spirit

TWENTY-THREE

That I May Know Him

I believe the Lord would be pleased for us to read from the third chapter of Philippians, beginning with verse three, and seven through fourteen:

> For we are the circumcision, which worship God in the spirit, and rejoice in Christ Jesus, and have no confidence in the flesh.... But what things were gain to me, those I counted loss for Christ. Yea doubtless, and I count all things *but* loss for the excellency of the knowledge of Christ Jesus my Lord: for whom I have suffered the loss of all things, and do count them *but* dung, that I may win Christ. And be found in him, not having mine own righteousness, which is of the law, but that which is through the faith of Christ, the righteousness which is of God by faith: That I may know him, and the power of his resurrection, and the fellowship of his sufferings, being made conformable unto his death; if by any means I might attain unto the resurrection of the dead. Not as though I had already attained, either were already perfect: but I fol-

low after, if that I may apprehend that for which also I am apprehended of Christ Jesus. Brethren, I count not myself to have apprehended: but *this* one thing I *do*, forgetting those things which are behind, and reaching forth unto those things which are before, I press toward the mark for the prize of the high calling of God in Christ Jesus.

One can only pray for God to enlarge these visions today. I believe that God will, by his power, bring us into likeminded, precious faith to believe all the Scriptures say. The Scriptures are at such depths that one could never enter into those things without being enlarged in God. Beloved, one thing is certain this morning: God can do it. "All things that *pertain* unto life and godliness" (2 Peter 1:3b) are in the pursuit, with a faith that will not have a dim sight, but clears everything and claims all that God puts before it.

I pray that God would so unfold to us the depths of his righteousness that we may no longer be poor, but very rich in God by his Spirit. Beloved, it is God's thought to make us all very rich in grace and in the knowledge of God through our Lord Jesus Christ. We have before us this morning a message which is full of heights and depths, lengths and breadths; a message which came out of brokenness of spirit, the loss of all things, enduring all things; a message where flesh and all that pertains to this world had to come to nothing.

LIFTED BY THE SPIRIT

We can worship God only in the Spirit. God can take us onto this spiritual plane with himself that we may be grounded in all knowledge, and so settled on all spiritual lines till from that place we will always be lifted by God. Human beings try to lift themselves, but there is no inspiration in that. But when we are lifted by the Spirit, when we are taken on with God, everything comes into perfect harmony and we go forth right on to victory. That is a grand place to come to, where we "rejoice in Christ Jesus and have no confidence in the flesh."

Paul adds, "Though I might also have confidence in the flesh" (vs 4). Paul had kept the law blameless, but I find another holds him in the same place. Oh, that is the greatest of all, when the Lord Jesus holds the reins. Then we no longer have anything to boast about because all our perfection according to law-keeping and law-abiding ceases. Oh, it is beautiful as we gaze upon the perfect Jesus! Jesus so outstrips everything else. For this reason Paul felt that everything must become as dross, whatever he was, whatever he had been. There was no help for him in anything. There is no help for us except on the lines of helplessness and nothingness.

I know nothing like a travail in the Spirit. Oh, it is a burden till you are relieved. I have had those days, and I have had it this morning, but now God is lifting the travail. And I say, brother, sister, unless God brings us into a place of brokenness of spirit, unless he remolds us in the great plan of his will for us, the best of us shall utterly fail. But when we are absolutely taken in hand by the Almighty God, he makes even weakness to be strength. He makes even that barren, helpless, groaning cry come forth so that men and women are born in the travail. There is a place where the helplessness is touched by the almightiness of God and where you come out shining as gold tried in the fire.

Oh, beloved, I see there is no hope for pentecostals except on broken conditions. It was there on the cross that our Lord died with a broken heart. Pentecost came out of jeering and sneering, and a sip of vinegar, and a smite with a rod, and a judgment that was passed apart from him, and a cross that he had to bear. But, glory to God, Pentecost rings out this morning through the Word. "It is finished" (John 19:30) for us! And now because it is finished, we can take the same place that Christ took and rise out of that death into majestic glory with the resurrection touch of heaven that shall make people know after this day that God has done something for us.

A DAILY REVIVAL IN OUR HEARTS

Every day there must be a revival touch in our hearts. Every day must change us after his fashion. We are to be made new all the time. There is no such thing as having all grace and knowledge. There is a beginning, and God would have us begin in all these beatitudes of power and never cease, but rise and rise and go on to perfection.

Let us look at some beatitudes that God wants us to reach this day. "But what things were gain to me, those I counted loss for Christ. Yea doubtless, and I count all things *but* loss for the excellency of the knowledge of Christ Jesus my Lord: for whom I have suffered the loss of all things, and do count them *but* dung, that I may win Christ" (Philippians 3:7-8). Also we turn to Hebrews 10:32: "But call to remembrance the former days, in which, after ye were illuminated, ye endured a great fight of afflictions." I am positive that no one can attain likemindedness on these lines except by the illumination of the Spirit.

God has been speaking to me over and over again that I must press all the people to receive the baptism of the Holy Ghost, because I see in this blessed gift unlimited grace and the endurance in that revelation by the Spirit. The excellency of Christ can never be understood except by illumination. And I find the Holy Ghost is that great illuminator who makes me understand all the depths of God. I must witness Christ.

Jesus said to Thomas: "Thomas, because thou hast seen me, thou hast believed: blessed *are* they that have not seen, and *yet* have believed" (John 20:29). So I can see there is a revelation which brings me into touch with God and allows me to see right into the fulness of our Head, Jesus Christ.

As Paul saw the depths and heights of the grandeur of God,

he longed that he might win him. Before his conversion, in his passion and zeal, Paul would do anything to bring Christians to death. And that passion that was in him raged like a mighty lion. As he was going on the way to Damascus, he heard the voice of Jesus saying, "Saul, Saul, why persecutest thou me?" (Acts 9:4). What broke him up was the tenderness of God.

Beloved, it is always God's tenderness over our weakness and over our depravity that breaks us as well. If somebody came along to thwart us, we would stand in our corner, but when we come to one who forgives us all, we know not what to do. Oh, to win him, my brother and sister!

There are a thousand things in the nucleus of a human heart which need softening a thousand times a day. There are things in us that, unless God shows us the excellency of the knowledge of him, will never be broken and brought to ashes. But God will do it. Not merely to be saved, but to be saved a thousand times over! Oh, this transforming regeneration by the power of the Spirit of the living God makes me see there is a place to win him, that I may stand complete in that place. As Jesus was, so am I to be. The Scriptures declare it; it shall be.

"And be found in him, not having mine own righteousness, which is of the law, but that which is through the faith of Christ, the righteousness which is of God by faith" (Philippians 3:9). Not depending upon my works but upon the faithfulness of God, being able under all circumstances to be hidden in him, covered by the almighty presence of God!

The Scriptures declare unto us that we are in Christ and Christ is in God. What is able to move us from the place of omnipotent power? "*Shall* tribulation, or distress, or persecution, or famine, or nakedness, or peril, or sword?" (Romans 8:35b). Ah, no! Shall life, or death, or principalities, or powers? No. The answer is found in verse 37: "We are more than conquerors through him who loved us."

Oh, but I must be found in him! There is a place of seclusion, a place of rest and faith in Jesus where nothing else compares.

Jesus came to his disciples on the water and they were terrified, but he said, "It is I; be not afraid" (Matthew 14:27b). Beloved, he is always there. He is there in the storm as well as in the peace; he is there in the adversity. When shall we know he is there? When we are "found in him," not having our own work, our own plan, but resting in the omnipotent plan of God.

THE PLACE OF BOLDNESS

Oh, is it possible for the child of God to fail? It is not possible. "He that keepeth thee will not slumber" (Psalm 121:3). He shall watch over you continually. Oh, but we must be found *in him*. I know there is a shelter in Jesus which opens to us this morning.

My brother, my sister, you have been nearly weighed down with troubles. They have almost crushed you. Sometimes you have thought you would never get out of this place of difficulty, but you have no idea that behind the whole thing, God has been working a plan greater than all. "That I may know him, and the power of his resurrection" (Philippians 3:10a).

Jesus said to Martha, "I am the resurrection, and the life" (John 11:25a). Today is a resurrection day. We must know the resurrection of his power in brokenness of spirit. Oh, to know this power of resurrection, to know the rest of faith! To know the supplanting of his power in you this morning! To make you see that any one of us, without exception, can reach these beatitudes in the Spirit.

Ah, there is something different between *saying* you have faith and then being pressed into a tight corner and *proving* that you have faith. If you dare believe, it shall be done according to your faith. "What things soever ye desire, when ye pray, believe that ye receive *them,* and ye shall have *them*" (Mark 11:24).

Jesus is the resurrection and the life. God help us to attain to it. We attain to it in that knowledge that he who came forth is to make us white as snow, pure and holy as he, that we may go with boldness unto the throne of grace. Boldness is in his holiness. Boldness is in his righteousness. Boldness is in his truth. You cannot have the boldness of faith if you are not pure. What a blessed word follows, "the fellowship of his sufferings" (Philippians 3:10b). Remember, unless that fellowship touches us, we shall never have much power.

What helped Jesus when he saw the withered hand, when he saw the woman who could in no wise help herself? When the Spirit of the Lord blows upon you, you will be broken down and then built up. Jesus came forth in the glory of the Father, filled with all the fulness of God. It was the thought of God before the foundation of the world, with such love over all the fearful, helpless human race, with all its blackness and hideousness of sin, and God loved us and brought redemption.

May God give us such fellowship with his sufferings that when we see the person afflicted with cancer, we will pray right through until the roots are struck dead. When we see the crooked and helpless woman or man, so infirm, that God will give us a compassion and a fellowship with them that shall undo their heavy burdens and set them free. How often we have missed the victory because we did not have the Lord's compassion at the needed moment. We failed to go through with a broken heart.

HAVE WE TRULY DIED?

Is there anything more? Oh, yes, we must see the next thing. "Being made conformable unto his death." Jesus taught that "except a corn of wheat fall into the ground and die, it abideth alone: but if it die, it bringeth forth much fruit" (John 12:24). God wants you to see that unless you are dead indeed, unless you come to a perfect crucifixion, unless you die with Jesus, you are not in the fellowship of his sufferings.

May God move upon us in this life to bring us into an absolute death—not merely to talk about it, not assuming it, but really dying to ourselves so that God's life may indeed be made manifest. Paul said, "I count not myself to have apprehended: but *this* one thing I *do:* forgetting those things which are behind, and reaching forth unto those things which are before, I press toward the mark for the prize of the high calling of God in Christ Jesus" (Philippians 3:13-14).

Paul had just said that he was following after to attain that for which he had been taken captive by Christ Jesus. And I believe God wants us to be of the same mind, that we too may be able to say, "I know I have died." The Lord wants us to understand that we must come to a place where our natural life ceases, and by the power of God we rise into a life where God rules, where he reigns.

Do you long to know him? Do you long to be found in him? Your longing shall be satisfied today. This is a day of putting on and being clothed upon in God. I ask you to fall in the presence of God. Yield to his mighty power and obey the Spirit.

THE MAN AND HIS MESSAGE

From *Triumphs of Faith* (Oakland, California), March 1927, pages 55-59. Revised and condensed by Carrie Judd Montgomery.

When he taught about being used of God, Wigglesworth hardly expected that the Holy Spirit would control the lives of everyone in exactly the same manner. Each person is different, as different as the snowflakes or the grains of sand. Believers are also part of the body, each member with a different function. Not even Wigglesworth wanted his hearers to be clones, although he did expect them to gain a new appreciation of what was available to believers. Above all, he wanted them to move from unbelief, or a passive faith, to an active faith. He viewed that kind of a change as "God taking us from the ordinary into the extraordinary, from the human into the divine, and making us after the image of his Son."

TWENTY-FOUR

Living Epistles of Christ

I want to read to you this morning from the third chapter of 2 Corinthians. We have here one of those high-water marks of very deep things of God in the Spirit. I believe the Lord will reveal to us these truths as our hearts are open and responsive to the Spirit's teaching. The Lord of hosts camps round about us this morning with "songs of deliverance" that we may see face-to-face the glory of his grace in a new way. For God has not brought us into cunningly devised fables, but in these days is rolling away the mists and clouds and every difficulty that we may understand the mind and will of God.

If we are going to receive the best from God, there must be in this meeting a spiritual desire, an open ear, an understanding heart. The veil must be lifted. We must see that God has nothing for us on the old lines. The new plan, the new revelation, the new victories are before us. New ground must be gained; supernatural things must be attained. All carnal things and evil powers and spiritual wickedness must be dethroned.

I will dwell for a few moments on these beautiful words taken from the Scriptures which I have read to you: "Ye are our epistle written in our hearts, known and read of all men: *Forasmuch as you are* manifestly declared to be the epistle of Christ ministered by us, written not with ink, but with the Spirit of the living God; not in tables of stone, but in fleshy tables of the heart" (2 Corinthians 3:2-3).

What an ideal position in that God's glory is being revealed, that the Word of God is becoming an expressed purpose in life, until the Word begins to live in these Christians and they become epistles of Christ. How true this position was in the life of Paul when he came to the climax and said, "I am crucified with Christ: nevertheless I live; yet not I, but Christ liveth in me: and the life which I now live in the flesh I live by faith of the Son of God, who loved me, and gave himself for me" (Galatians 2:20).

How can Christ live in you? There is no way for Christ to live in you except by the manifested Word in you and through you, declaring every day that you are a living epistle of the Word of God. It is the living Christ. It is the divine likeness of God. It is the express image of him. The Word is the only factor that works within you and brings forth these glories of identification between you and Christ. Everything that comes to us must be quickened by the Spirit. Remember that "the letter killeth, but the spirit giveth life" (2 Corinthians 3:66). We must have life in everything.

Who knows how to pray only as the Spirit prays? What kind of prayer does the Spirit pray? The Spirit always brings to our remembrance the mind of the Scriptures and brings forth all our cry and our need better than our words. The Spirit takes the Word of God and brings our heart, and mind, and soul, and cry, and need into the presence of God.

The Spirit prays only according to the will of God, and the will of God is in all the Word of God. When we have entered in with God into the mind of the Spirit, we will find that God changes our hearts. And when God reaches into the depths of our hearts, he purifies every intention and desire. We are told in the Word that it is joy unspeakable and full of glory.

NOT IN TABLES OF STONE

Beloved, it is true that the commandments were written on tables of stone. Moses had a heart full of joy because God had shown him a plan where Israel could partake of great things through these commandments. But now God says, "Not in tables of stone" which made the face of Moses to shine with great joy. Deeper than that, more wonderful than that, his commandments are now written in our hearts. We know his deep love and compassion, the moving of eternity rolling in and bringing God in.

Oh, beloved, let God the Holy Ghost have his way today in thus unfolding to us the grandeur of his glory. "Not that we are sufficient of ourselves to think any thing as of ourselves; but our sufficiency *is* of God" (2 Corinthians 3:5). Ah, it is lovely! These verses are too deep to pass over.

Beloved, that is a climax of divine exaltation which is so different from human exaltation. We want to get to a place where we are beyond trusting in ourselves. Beloved, there is so much failure in self-assurances. We must never have anything in the human that we rest upon. Our trust is in God. When we have no confidence to trust in ourselves, but when our whole trust rests upon the authority of the mighty God, he has promised to be with us at all times and to make our paths straight and to remove the mountains.

Ah, lover of souls! We have no confidence in the flesh. Our confidence can only be in the one who never fails, in the one who knows the end from the beginning, in the one who is able to come in at the midnight hour as easily as at noonday, and make the night and day alike to the person who rests completely in the will of God, knowing that all things work together for good to those who love him.

Let us continue with verses seven and eight in holy thoughtfulness: "But if the ministration of death, written *and* engraven in stones, was glorious, so that the children of Israel could not steadfastly behold the face of Moses for the glory of his counte-nance: which *glory* was to be done away: How shall not the min-istration of the spirit be rather glorious?"

We cannot define, or separate, or deeply investigate and unfold this holy plan of God unless we have the life of God, the thought of God, the Spirit of God, and the revelation of God. The Word of truth is pure, spiritual, and divine. We must know that the baptism of the Spirit immerses us into an intensity of zeal, into a likeness to Jesus, to make us into pure, molten metal, so hot for God that it travels like oil from vessel to vessel.

There is not a natural thought that can be of any use here. There is not a thing that is carnal, earthly, natural, that can live if one has this experience. The human has to die eternally because there is no other plan for a Spirit-baptized soul. God help us to see that it is possible to be filled with the letter of the Word without being filled with the Spirit. We may be filled with knowledge without having divine knowledge. No one is able to walk this way without being in the Spirit. We must live in the Spirit, and realize all the time that we are growing in that same ideal of our Master, in season and out of season, always behold-ing the face of Jesus.

THE MAN AND HIS MESSAGE

Originally titled "Epistles of Christ" from *Triumphs of Faith* (Oakland, California), April 1926, pages 86-88. Revised and con-densed by Carrie Judd Montgomery. Wigglesworth sometimes preached at Mrs. Montgomery's interdenominational meetings held in the center of Oakland. Although he appreciated his minis-terial credentials with the United States Assemblies of God dur-ing the 1920s, Wigglesworth never made denominational membership a basis for fellowship. He gladly worshiped with all believers, and everyone was always welcome at his meetings.[1]

TWENTY-FIVE

Empty Vessels Filled by the Spirit

God does not dwell in temples made by hands but in poor and contrite hearts. "God *is* a Spirit: and they that worship him must worship *him* in spirit and in truth" (John 4:23-24).

The church is the body of Christ. Its worship is a heart-worship, a longing to come into the presence of God. He wants us to come to a place of undisturbed rest and peace. Only simplicity will bring us there. Jesus said, "Except ye... become as little children, ye shall not enter into the kingdom of heaven" (Matthew 18:3). This means not to have the child's mind but the child's spirit of meekness, gentleness. It is the only place to meet God. He will give us that place of worship.

How my heart cries out for a deep vision of God. The world cannot produce it. A place where we see the Lord—that when we pray, we know God hears. Asking God and believing for the answer, having no fear, but a living faith to come into the presence of God. "In thy presence *is* fulness of joy; at thy right hand *there are* pleasures for evermore" (Psalm 16:11). God is looking for a people in whom he can reveal himself.

I used to have a tremendous temper, turning red with passion. My whole nature was outside God in that way. God knew his child could never be of service to the world unless he was wholly sanctified. I was difficult to please at the table. My wife was a good cook, but there was always something wrong. After God sanctified me, however, I heard her testify in a meeting that from that time on I was pleased with everything. I had men working for me and wanted to be a good testimony to them. One day they waited after work was over and said, "We would like that spirit you have."

It is our human spirit that has to be controlled by the Holy Spirit. There is a place where Christ reigns in the body; then all is well. This word is full of stimulation as we are brought by faith into a place of grace where all may see us being created anew. If you believe, you can be sons of God—in likeness, character, spirit, longings, acts, until all will know you are a son of God.

The Spirit of God can change your nature. God is Creator. His Word is creative. And as you believe, a creative power is changing your whole nature. You can reach this attitude only by faith. No one can change himself. The God of almightiness spreads his covering over you, saying, "I am able to do all things and all things are possible to those who believe."

THE BRIDEGROOM IS PREPARING THE BRIDE

The old nature is so difficult to manage. You have been ashamed of it many a time, but the Lord himself will come. He says, "Come unto me, and I will give you rest, peace, strength. I will change you. I will operate upon you by my power, making you a new creation, if you will believe."

Take your burden to the Lord and leave it there. "Learn of me; for I am meek and lowly in heart: and ye shall find rest unto your souls" (Matthew 11:29). The world has no rest; it is full of trouble. But in Christ is peace which passes understanding, with an inward flow of divine power changing your nature until you can live, move, and act in the power of God.

"Therefore the world knoweth us not, because it knew him not" (1 John 3:1b). What does this word mean? I have lived in one house over fifty years. I have preached from my own doorstep, and all around know me. They know me when they need someone to pray, when there is trouble, when they need help. But at Christmastime when they call their friends, would they call me? No! Why? Because they would say, "He is sure to want a prayer meeting, but we want to finish up with a dance."

Wherever Jesus came, sin was revealed and human beings don't like sin revealed. Sin separates from God forever. You are in a good place when you weep before God, repenting over the least thing. If you have spoken unkindly, you realize it was not like the Lord. Your keen conscience has taken you to prayer. It is a wonderful thing to have a keen conscience. It is when we are close to God that our hearts are revealed. God intends for us to live in purity, seeing him all the time.

"Beloved, now are we the sons of God, and it doth not yet appear what we shall be: but we know that, when he shall appear, we shall be like him; for we shall see him as he is. And every man that hath this hope in him purifieth himself, even as he is pure" (1 John 3:2-3). It is the hope of the church: the bridegroom coming for the bride. He has suffered for us, was buried for us, is risen for us, is jealous for us. How we should love him! He is coming again, and he wants us to be ready.

The world does not know us, but we are sons of God with power. No one who sins has power. Sin makes a person weak. Remember this: sin dethrones, but purity strengthens. Temptation is not sin, but the devil is a liar and tries to take away our peace. You must live in the Word of God. There is now no condemnation. Who can condemn you? Christ has died. He won't condemn you. He died to save you. Don't condemn yourself. If there is anything wrong, come to the blood.

"If we walk in the light, as he is in the light, we have fellowship one with another, and the blood of Jesus Christ his Son cleanseth us from all sin" (1 John 1:7). Jesus was manifested to destroy the works of the devil. We can come into a new experience with God where he creates in our hearts such a love for Jesus that we are living in a new realm: sons of God with power, filled with all the fulness of God.

Before leaving home I received a wire asking if I would go to Liverpool. There was a woman with cancer and gallstones. If I know God is sending me, my faith rises. The woman said, "I have no hope." God said to me, "Establish her in the fact of the new birth." When she had the assurance that her sin was gone and she was born again, she said, "That is everything to me. Cancer is nothing now that I have Jesus." The battle was won. God delivered her and she was free and soon up and dressed, and happy in Jesus.

Life and immortality are ours in the gospel. This is our inheritance through the blood of Jesus, life forevermore. Believe and the Lord will transmit life through you, that you may be waiting for his coming and witnessing unto him.

THE MAN AND HIS MESSAGE

Originally titled "Lives Controlled by the Spirit of Christ" from the *Pentecostal Evangel* (Springfield, Missouri), April 26, 1941, page 4. Although World War II prevented Wigglesworth from traveling, his sermons continued to circulate in his books and in Christian magazines. How can one be controlled by the Holy Spirit? This is possible, Wigglesworth preached, when believers yield themselves to Christ as empty vessels so they can be filled with the Holy Spirit (Acts 2:4).

TWENTY-SIX

Rising into the Heavenlies

Whenever in the history of the world there has been a divine revelation—God coming forth in some manifestation of his Spirit—antagonism and opposition with persecution have been directed toward those who received such manifestations or revelations. In the old dispensation, as well as in the new, when the Spirit of God has been moving mightily, trouble and difficulty soon follow.

Why is this? It is because there are some things very much against the revelation of God and the operation of the Holy Spirit. First, there is the flesh, the natural man, because "the carnal mind *is* enmity against God" (Romans 8:7a). The very fact that human beings throughout the world, as a rule, are opposed to the working of God provides firm evidence of the truth of this statement of Scripture.

Second, out of the natural man's enmity against God grows the opposition of the world, which is the mass of those antagonistic individuals put together. Our Lord Jesus Christ has made it unmistakably plain to all his followers for all time that the world is contrary to him and to his kingdom. He said concerning his disciples, "I have given them thy word; and the world hath hated them, because they are not of the world, even as I am not of the world" (John 17:14).

Third, the devil and all his evil hosts are also arrayed against every manifestation of God. The devil is "the prince of this world" (John 16:11); and he is "the spirit that now worketh in the children of disobedience" (Ephesians 2:2b). All these are opposed to God and his working, but they can never defeat his purposes. So far as the human eye can see, God's cause is often in the minority; but viewed by those who have spiritual eyesight, "They that be with us *are* more than they that be with them" (2 Kings 6:16). So, as Elisha said to his servant, "Fear not." Wickedness may increase and abound; but when the Lord raises his banner over a saint, it is victory, even though the saint may seem to be in the minority.

PRIVILEGES OF THE ELECT

The Holy Ghost wants us to understand our privileges— "elect according to the foreknowledge of God the Father, through sanctification of the Spirit" (1 Peter 1:2a). This work of the "sanctification of the Spirit" (2 Thessalonians 2:13) does not refer to cleansing from sin. It refers to a higher order of redemptive work.

The blood of Jesus is all-powerful for cleansing; but when sin is gone, when we are clean and when we know we have the Word of God in us, and when the power of the Spirit is bringing everything to a place where we triumph over all evil, then comes a revelation through the Spirit. This revelation lifts us onto higher ground and unveils the fulness of the life of Christ within us in such a way that we are led on till we are "filled with all the fulness of God" (Ephesians 3:19a).

This is the sanctification of the Spirit. It is the great work for which the Spirit was given. This is the purpose for which God has called you. Whether you have accepted your election, whether you have proved yourself worthy of your election, whether you have allowed the Spirit to thus sanctify you, I do not know. But if you yield yourself to God and let his Holy Spirit have his way in your spirit to lead you into the will of God, as it is revealed in the Word of God, he will not fail to "do exceedingly abundantly above all that we ask or think" (Ephesians 3:20).

This word "elect" is a very precious word to me. It shows me that, before the world was, God planned to bring us into such glorious triumph and victory in Christ that "unto him [shall] be glory in the church by Christ Jesus throughout all ages, world without end. Amen" (Ephesians 3:21). Feed upon these words; let them sink into your heart. God has purposed to do for those in the church something which will redound to the glory of his name unto the endless ages.

This is the most solid ground for faith—that salvation is to be "to the praise of the glory of his grace" (Ephesians 1:6a). God has predetermined, has planned, has made full provision to accomplish this wondrous work in all who will not "frustrate the grace of God" (Galatians 2:21a). Some people pervert this blessed truth. They say, "Oh, well, you see, we are elected; we are all right." I know many who believe in that kind of election. They say they are elected to be saved; and they believe others are elected to be damned.

It is not true. *Everybody* is elected to be saved; whether they come into it or not is another thing. This perverted view of this precious truth makes souls indifferent to its great purpose, the "sanctification of the Spirit" (2 Thessalonians 2:13). This is one of the ways in which Satan opposes the work of God in the world—by perverting it, making it to appear to mean something that it does not mean, so that souls are kept from pressing on into the glorious purpose of God for which salvation was planned. That would be a poor salvation which did not deliver humanity from the thing which causes all the sorrow and trouble in this world: sin.

Notice again, this sanctification of the Spirit is "unto obedience and sprinkling of the blood of Jesus Christ" (1 Peter 1:2b). There is no sanctification if it is not sanctification unto obedience. There would be no trouble with any of us if we would all come definitely to the place where we understand and accept that word of our Lord Jesus when he said, "For their sakes I sanctify myself, that they also might be sanctified through the truth" (John 17:19). Jesus had just prayed, "Sanctify them through thy truth: thy word is truth" (vs 17).

SANCTIFICATION PRODUCES OBEDIENCE

When you come into the election of the sanctification of the Spirit, you will be obedient to everything revealed in that word. And in the measure that you are not obedient, you have not come into the sanctification of the Spirit. A little thing spoils many good things. People say, "Mr. So-and-so is very good, but..." "Mrs. So-and-so is excellent, but..." "Oh, you know that young man is progressing tremendously, but..."

There are no "buts" in the sanctification of the Spirit. "But" and "if" are gone, and it is "shall" and "I will" all the way through. Beloved, if there are any "buts" in your attitude toward this word of truth, it indicates that there is something unyielded to the Spirit. I pray that we may be willing to yield ourselves to the sanctification of the Spirit, that we may enter into the mind of God regarding this election and come into actual possession of it.

Perhaps to encourage you, it will be helpful to show you what election is, because there is no difficulty in proving whether you are elected or not. Why are you interested in this book? Is it because you have a desire for more of God? If so, it is God who has given you that desire; and God is drawing you unto himself.

If you have truly received Jesus as your Lord and Savior, it has been because the Father drew you to him; for he said, "No man can come to me, except the Father which hath sent me draw him" (John 6:44). And we may be sure that God will not go back on what he has begun to do; for our Lord Jesus added to the above, "And I will raise him up at the last day."

Also the apostle Paul says, in Philippians 1:6, "Being confident of this very thing, that he which hath begun a good work in you will perform *it* until the day of Jesus Christ." When I think of my own case, I recall that in my childhood I was strangely moved upon by the Spirit. At the age of eight years I was definitely saved; and at nine, I felt the Spirit come upon me just as when I spoke in tongues.

You may say of yourself, "When I was in sin, I was troubled." Thank God for it, for it was his Spirit that troubled you. It is a most blessed thought that we have a God of love, compassion, and grace, who wills not the death of one sinner. God has made it possible for all men and women to be saved, by causing Jesus, his well-beloved Son, to die for the sins of the whole world. It is true that he took our sins; it is true that he paid the price for the whole world; it is true that he gave himself as a ransom for many; it is true, beloved, it is true.

And you ask, "For whom?" "Whosoever will, let him take the water of life freely" (Revelation 22:17b). What about the others? It would have to be a refusal of the blood of Jesus; it would have to be a refusal to have Christ reign over them; that's it. It is "Whosoever will" on the one side, and "Whosoever won't" on the other side; and there are people in the world who won't. What is up with them? "The god of this world hath blinded the minds of them which believe not, lest the light of the glorious gospel of Christ, who is the image of God, should shine unto them" (2 Corinthians 4:4).

Through sanctification of the Spirit, according to this election, you will get to a place where you are not disturbed. There is a peace in the sanctification of the Spirit, because it is a place of revelation, of heavenly places into which you are brought. It is a place where God comes and makes himself known to you. And when you are face-to-face with God you receive a peace that passes all understanding, and which lifts you from state to state of inexpressible wonderment. Oh, it is wonderful!

THE CRUCIBLE OF FAITH

"Blessed *be* the God and Father of our Lord Jesus Christ, which according to his abundant mercy, hath begotten us again unto a lively hope by the resurrection of Jesus Christ from the dead" (1 Peter 1:3). This sanctification of the Spirit brings us into definite line with this wonderful "lively hope" of the glory of God.

A lively hope is exactly the opposite of something dead. A lively hope means movement. A lively hope means looking into what we hope for. A lively hope means pressing into that which is promised. A lively hope means keeping the vision. A lively hope sees Jesus coming. And you live in this lively hope. You are not trying to make yourself *feel* that you are believing. But this lively hope keeps you waiting, and ready, and filled with the joy of expectation of the coming of the King. Praise the Lord!

If the thought of the coming of the King is not such a lively hope to you, you need to search whether you have ever truly enthroned him as King over your own life. God has this in mind for you. There is real joy in the expectation of his coming; and there will be infinitely greater joy in the realization.

I trust that you will be so reconciled to God that not one thing will interfere with your having this lively hope. If you have any love for the world, this hope cannot be a lively hope to you; for his coming will mean the overthrow of this world. If there is in you the pride of life, this hope cannot be to you a lively hope; for every high thing will be brought low in that day (Isaiah 1).

Salvation is very much misunderstood. That which comes to

us in a moment of time, through believing, is only the beginning. Salvation is so wonderful, so mighty, so tremendous, that it goes on and on from one degree to another until there shall be nothing in us from which we need to be delivered—either in spirit, or soul, or mind, or body. Everything is ready so far as God is concerned, and is waiting for us to get ready to receive it.

Sin began in the spirit of humankind, and salvation must be wrought out there before there can be deliverance from the *consequences* of sin. In the meantime, if we rest our faith in the power of God, we will be "kept by the power of God through faith unto salvation ready to be revealed in the last time" (1 Peter 1:5).

We have no idea what God wants to do for us through trials and temptations. They do two things for us. When there is anything wrong in us which we are not recognizing, trials bring it to the surface, that we may see our need of God's salvation in this respect.

But why are even the most faithful of God's children tried and tempted? It is that their very faithfulness and loyalty and the purity of their faith may be made manifest, and "found unto praise and honour and glory at the appearing of Jesus Christ" (vs 7). Gold has to be tried with fire, and it is made more precious thereby. Your faith, Peter says, "[is] much more precious than of gold that perisheth" (vs 7).

One day I went to a certain place and a gentleman there said to me, "Would you like to see the purification of gold?" I said yes. So he got some gold and put it into a crucible, and put a blast of heat under it. First it became blood red, and then it changed and changed. Then the man took an instrument and passed it over the gold. It drew off something which was foreign to the gold. He did this several times, until every bit of that foreign substance was taken away.

Then he said to me, "Look!" And there we both saw our faces reflected in the gold! It was wonderful! My brother and sister, your faith is much more precious than gold that perishes.

As you are tried and tested in the fire, the Master is bringing the dross to the surface and taking it away—taking away all that hinders his image being seen in you, all that is not enduring, all that is not precious in his sight.

It is lovely to know that in times of misunderstanding—in times when you are in the right and yet are treated as though you were in the wrong—God is meeting you, blessing you, accomplishing something which will not only glorify his name but also be to your "praise and honour and glory at the appearing of Jesus Christ" (1 Peter 1:7b). So do not chafe or fret. Let the fire burn; it will do you good.

"Whom having not seen, ye love" (vs 8). Oh, how sweet! There is no voice and no touch so gentle, so soft, so full of tenderness as his. Is it possible to love him when we have not seen him? God will make it possible. And, "though now ye see *him* not, yet believing," he will enable you to "rejoice with joy unspeakable and full of glory" (vs 8). Rejoice! We have something glorious to rejoice over.

Oh, what a salvation God has provided for us in all our worthlessness and nothingness and helplessness! I entreat you from the Lord to be so reconciled to him that there will be no division between you and him. Will you give him preeminence in all things? Shall he not have his rightful place and decide for you the way and plan of your life? Beloved, when you allow him to decide for you, when you want nothing but his blessed will, when he is very Lord and sovereign of all, then you will have a foretaste of heaven all the time. The Lord bless you with grace to leave all and say, "I will follow you, Lord Jesus."

THE MAN AND HIS MESSAGE

From the *Pentecostal Evangel* (Springfield, Missouri), May 30, 1925, pages 2-3, 5. Smith Wigglesworth, who never tried to hide the fact that he enjoyed finely tailored suits and expensive shoes and traveled first-class, drew criticism from people who believed being spiritual meant living poor. "I'm not saving the Lord's money," he explained, "I'm saving the Lord's servant." He also said, "If the Lord doesn't look after me, it will be time to go back to plumbing."[1]

TWENTY-SEVEN

The Privileges of Sonship

I want to read one of those remarkable passages which are exhaustless, the third chapter of the First Epistle of John. We see here the attitude of believers, our inspiration, a place where we rest in faith. There we know that God has done something marvelous for us: he has taken us out of the world. Jesus said, "They are not of the world."

This is a great truth for us to understand. In this glorious position we say without fear of contradiction from our own hearts, or even from outside voices, "Beloved, now are we the sons of God" (vs 2). God wants us to be something more than ordinary people. When God lays hold of a person, he makes that person extraordinary in personality, power, unction, thought, and activity.

God has made us his sons and daughters. It is a divine plan. God has a great desire to utter these words in our hearts so that we may rise higher into our privileges, that we may be ambitious, that we may be covetous, so that nothing can satisfy us unless we come into line with God and claim all that belongs to us as his children.

Through the Word of God you may become a living epistle by the power of the Holy Ghost. You may have within you the incarnation of the personality of Christ's presence, until you know that you are God's children. You will have son-likeness, son-desires, son-expressions, son-activities. Beloved, this remarkable position awaits every soul in this place: to be so inhabited by Jesus that you become a living personality of God's ideal Son. This is very remarkable and very beautiful.

Many people believe that because they are in the natural, they are always to be in the place of weakness. But, beloved, your weakness must be swallowed up by the power of him who never failed. Every time that Jesus Christ was tried, he emerged victorious. "[He] was in all points tempted like as *we are, yet* without sin" (Hebrews 4:15b). Jesus was thus tempted and overcame in order that he might be able to succor all who are tempted and tried and oppressed in any way.

We are saved by the immensity of his power, the great inflow of his life, the almighty fulness of God. As the wonderful inhabiting of the Spirit comes into the human soul, he shakes the husks away, he shakes the mind. Oh, how many people lose out because the mind and the head were too big, the mind too active and too much in the natural. Therefore, God cannot get his way.

May God sweep through us today and show us that it is the *heart* that is moved by God. The mind is always secondary. When our whole lives are surged by the power of God, we become subjects of the Spirit of the living God and we are moved by the almightiness of God. Then we live and move and have our being in this flow of God's wonder-working power. "God *is* able to make all grace abound" (2 Corinthians 9:8a). He is able to so shake us through and through, to send a wind and blow the chaff away till it will never be seen anymore.

A RISING TIDE OF EXPECTANCY

"Beloved, now are we the sons of God" (1 John 3:2a). I do not want to leave this subject until I feel that God has given you a rising tide of expectancy, an adaptability within your soul which will bring you into the very place God has made for you. This is as easy as possible if you can touch him by faith this morning.

I can understand now more clearly than ever the twenty-fourth psalm: "Lift up your heads, O ye gates" (vs 7). There are human gates, human hindrances, human thoughts, human trying. "Lift up your heads, O ye gates; and be ye lifted up, ye everlasting doors; and the King of glory shall come in."

If he comes in, what a wonderful Jesus! "Ah," you say, "he is in." Beloved, I believe if God could only get fully into your heart you would be so far out, you would never get in anymore. Who dares believe God this morning? Who dares claim the rights of sonship? What are the rights of the sons and daughters of God? Absolutely the position of rest, the position of faith, perfect trust, perfect habitation, no disturbance, peace like a river.

All the great things of God that come to us with such revelation can only come as we are first unclothed and then clothed by our Father, so that our nakedness disappears. Nakedness is everything that coincides with worldly evil. If you can be attracted by anything earthly, you have missed the great association that God has for you. If it is your ranch, your bank, any human thing, if it can distract you from God, you are not a son in this respect.

"Beloved, now are we the sons of God" (1 John 3:2a). Sonship! What is the reality of it? God gives it as clear as anything. If sonship, heirship; if heirs, then joint heirs. But look at the tremendous, gigantic power behind sonship. Son, power, joint power, all power. Dare you let the power of God make you see your inheritance in the Spirit? Nay, something better than that! Oh, the joyfulness, the expressiveness, the inward law, the divine inflow, the habitation of the Spirit, God in the soul making the whole body cry out for the living God! Glory! Glory! Glory!

Do you want God? Do you want fellowship in the Spirit? Do you want to walk with him? Do you want communion with him? God says, "I will dwell in them, and walk in *them*" (2 Corinthians 6:16b). "I will sup with you and you with me." This is attaining to a spiritual maturity, a fulness of Christ, a place where God becomes the chosen Father and the Holy Ghost has his rightful place as never before. The Spirit cries, "Abba, Father." Oh, it is wonderful! May God the Holy Ghost grant to us this morning that richness of his pleasure, that unfolding of his will, that consciousness of his beaming countenance upon us.

IS YOUR SOUL ON THE WING?

There is now no condemnation. The law of the Spirit of life in Christ Jesus makes us free from the law of sin and death. God has shown us different aspects of the Spirit. He has shown us the pavilion of splendor. He has shown us the power of the relationship of sonship. Sons of God may speak and it is done. They may bind things that are loose, and loose things that are bound.

Beloved, it is impossible to estimate the loving-kindness of God or the measureless mind of God while in our finite condition. When we come into likemindedness with God, we begin to see what God has for us in the Word. This is an exhaustless subject, but I pray God that he may make you an exhaustless people.

Let us pray: "O God, come to me and make me so that it is not a possibility for me to ever be satisfied except as I have a quenchless thirst for the living God."

There it is, beloved. "Now are we the sons of God" (1 John

3:2a). If you are there, you can take a step further; but if you are not there, you may hear but not cross over. If you hear in faith, the word shall profit, but there is a hearing not mixed with faith which shall not profit. You can hear this word on the lines of faith: "Beloved, now are we the sons of God, and it doth not yet appear what we shall be: but we know that, when he shall appear, we shall be like him; for we shall see him as he is" (1 John 3:2).

If God can get you into the right position today, tomorrow will be filled with further illumination of God's position for you. Dare you come into the place of omnipotence? Of wonderment? Dare you step into line with God's possibility and say, "I am ready for all you have for me"?

It will mean a clean life, it will mean a separated life, it will disjoin you from everything. It will mean that you are so divinely separated that you can say good-bye to the world. God would have me herald like a great trumpet call, so that it might sound forth in every heart: God's design is to bring you to the place where you will be a son clothed with the power of gifts and graces, ministries and operations, to bring you unto glory, clothed with the majesty of heaven. For he shall bring many sons and daughters unto glory—unto son-likeness, son-perfection.

Oh, this is like heaven to me! My very body is filled with the glory of heaven this morning. Beloved, seeing these things are so, what manner of persons ought we to be in looking, in hasting, and in keeping our eyes upon him, that we may be ready for the rapture?

Let me give you this word if you can receive it: "As he is, so are we in this world" (1 John 4:17b). What a wonderful word! Who dares to believe it? God alone can take each one of us on to such heights and depths and lengths and breadths in the Spirit. Brother, sister, are you prepared to go all the way? Are you willing for your heart to have only one attraction? Are you willing for Christ to become your bridegroom? For I understand that the more bridelike we are, the more we love to hear the Bridegroom's voice. And the less bridelike we are, the less we long for his word.

If you cannot rest without the Word, if it becomes your meat day and night, if you eat it, drink of it, his life will be in you. And when he appears, you will go to meet him. How many are prepared to meet the King? Prepared to yield to his call? Yield to his will? Yield to his desire? How many will say, "At all costs I will go through"? Are you determined? Is your soul on the wing? Come forward and make a full consecration to God and get right into his presence.

THE MAN AND HIS MESSAGE

From *Triumphs of Faith* (Oakland, California), August 1924, pages 178-81. Preached at the Pentecostal Camp Meeting, Berkeley, California. Abridged by Carrie Judd Montgomery and originally issued by Glad Tidings Temple, San Francisco.

Wigglesworth saw everyone as a person for whom Christ died, and all of God's sons and daughters were equal in his sight. "Race distinction was a thing unknown to him," his son-in-law, James Salter, wrote. "Black, red, yellow, all sought his ministry and all were blessed by his prayers and his gifts. He ignored social distinctions in his ministry, and he could be very severe on anyone who sought private claims on his attention on such grounds."[1]

TWENTY-EIGHT

Count It All Joy

James addressed his letter to "the twelve tribes which are scattered abroad" (James 1:1b). Only one like the Master could stand and say, "My brethren, count it all joy when ye fall into divers temptations" (vs 2). How could James write, "Count it all joy"? When they were scattered everywhere! Driven to their wit's end! Persecuted!

The Scriptures say that "they wandered in deserts, and *in* mountains, and *in* dens and caves of the earth" (Hebrews 11:38). His people were scattered abroad, but God was with them. It does not matter where you are if God is with you. He who is for you is a million times more than all who can be against you.

Oh, if we could by the grace of God see that the beatitudes of God's divine power come to us with such sweetness, whispering to us, "Be still, my child. All is well." Only be still and see the salvation of the Lord. Oh, what would happen if we learned the secret to ask only once and believe? What an advantage it would be if we could only come to a place where we knew that everything is within our reach. God wants us to see that every obstacle can be moved away.

God brings us into a place where there are difficulties, where there is no pleasure, where there are hard corners, where everything is so difficult. You know there are no possibilities on the human side—God must do it. All these places are of God's ordering. God allows trials, difficulties, temptations, and perplexities to come right along our path, but there is not a temptation or trial which can come to us but that God has a way out. *You* do not have a way out; it is *God* who can bring you through!

A lot of saints want me to pray for their nervous system. I guarantee there is not a person in the whole world who could be nervous if they understood the fourth chapter of the First Epistle of John. Let us read verses sixteen to eighteen: "And we have known and believed the love that God hath to us. God is love; and he that dwelleth in love dwelleth in God, and God in him. Herein is our love made perfect, that we may have boldness in the day of judgment: because as he is, so are we in this world. There is no fear in love; but perfect love casteth out fear: because fear hath torment. He that feareth is not made perfect in love."

Let me tell you what perfect love is: he who believes that Jesus is the Son of God overcomes the world. What is the evidence and assurance of salvation? Believing in the heart on the Lord Jesus. Every expression of love is in the heart. When you begin to breathe out your heart to God in affection, your very being, your whole self, desires him. Perfect love means that Jesus has gotten a grip on your intentions, desires, and thoughts and purified everything. Perfect love cannot fear.

FRESH CLAY IN THE POTTER'S HANDS

What God wants is to impregnate us with his Word. His Word is a living truth. I would pity a believer who has gone a whole week without temptation. Why? Because God only tries those who are worthy. You might be passing through difficulties. Trials are rising, darkness is appearing, and everything is becoming so dense you cannot see through it. Hallelujah! God is seeing you through. He is a God of deliverance, a God of power. Oh, he is near to save if you will only believe. He can anoint you with fresh oil; he can make your cup run over. Jesus is the balm of Gilead; yes, the Rose of Sharon.

I believe that God, the Holy Ghost, wants to bring us into line with such perfection of beatitude, of beauty, that we shall say, "Lord, Lord, though you slay me, yet will I trust you." When the hand of God is upon you and the clay is fresh in the Potter's hands, the vessel will be made perfect as you are pliable. Only melted gold is minted; only moistened clay is molded; only softened wax receives the seal; only broken, contrite hearts receive the mark as the Potter turns us on his wheel—shaped and burnt to take and keep the mark, the mold, the stamp of God's pure gold.

God can put the stamp on this morning. He can mold you afresh. He can change the vision. He can remove the difficulty. The Lord of Hosts is in your midst and is waiting for your affection. Remember his question: "Simon, *son* of Jonas, lovest thou me more than these?" (John 21:15b).

God never lets the chastening rod fall upon anything except that which is marring the vessel. If there is anything in you which is not yielded and bent to the plan of the Almighty, you cannot preserve that which is spiritual only in part. When the Spirit of the Lord gets perfect control, then we begin to be changed from glory to glory by the expression of God's light in our human frame. And the whole of the body begins to have the fulness of his life manifested in us until God enables us to believe all things.

Brother, sister, if God brings you into oneness and the fellowship with the most high God, your nature will quiver in his presence. But he can chase away all the defects, all the unrest, all the unfaithfulness, all the wavering. And he can establish you with such strong consolation that you can just rest there in the Holy Ghost by the power of God—ready to be revealed. God invites us to higher heights and deeper depths.

> Make me better, make me purer,
> By the fire which refines,
> Where the breath of God is sweeter,
> Where the brightest glory shines.
> Bring me higher up the mountain
> Into fellowship with thee,
> In thy light I'll see the fountain,
> And the blood that cleanses me.

A NEW VISION

I am realizing very truly these days that there is a sanctification of the Spirit where the thoughts are holy, where the life is beautiful, with no blemish. As you come closer into the presence of God, the Spirit wafts revelations of his holiness till he shows us a new plan for the present and the future. The heights and depths, the breadth, the lengths of God's inheritance for us are truly wonderful.

We read in Romans 8:10, "And if Christ *be* in you, the body *is* dead because of sin; but the Spirit *is* life because of righteousness." Oh, what a vision, beloved! "The body is dead" because sin is being judged, being destroyed. The whole body is absolutely put to death. And because of that position we partake of his righteousness and behold his beauty. The Spirit is life, freedom, joy. The Spirit lifts the soul into the presence of heaven. Ah, this is glorious.

"Count it all joy when ye fall into divers temptations" (James 1:2). Perhaps you have been counting it all sadness until now. Never mind, you turn the scale and you will get a lot out of it, more than ever you had before. Tell it to Jesus now. Express your inward heart throbbings to him.

He knows it all, he knows it all,
My Father knows, he knows it all.
The bitter tears, how fast they fall,
He knows, my Father knows it all.

Sometimes I change that song. And I would like to sing it as I change it, because there are two sides to it:

The joy he gives that overflows,
He knows, my Father knows it all.

Ah, yes, the bitterness may come at night, but joy will come in the morning. Hallelujah! So many believers never look up. Jesus lifted up his eyes and said, "Father, I thank thee that thou hast heard me" (John 11:41b). Then he cried with a loud voice, "Lazarus, come forth" (vs 43).

Beloved, God wants us to have some resurrection touch about us. We may enter into things that will bring us sorrow and trouble, but through them God will bring us to a deeper knowledge of himself. Never use your human plan when God speaks his word. You have your cue from an almighty source which has all the resources, which never fades away. His coffers are past measuring, abounding with extravagances of abundance, waiting to be poured out upon us.

Hear what the Scripture says: "God... giveth to all *men* liberally, and upbraideth not" (James 1:5b). The almighty hand of God comes to our weakness and says, "If you dare to trust me and will not waver, I will abundantly satisfy you out of the treasure house of the Most High."

"And upbraids not." What does it mean? God forgives, he supplies, he opens the door into his fulness and makes us know that he has done it all. When you come to him again, he gives you another overflow without measure, an expression of a father's love. Who wants something from God? He can satisfy every need. He satisfies the hungry with good things.

I ask you in the name of Jesus, will you cast all your care upon him? "For he cares for you." I am in great need this morning; I do want an overflow. Come on, beloved, let us weep together. I believe a real weeping would be good for us. You are in a poor way if you cannot weep. I do thank God for my tears. They help me. I do like to weep in the presence of God. God will help us. Glory to God. How he meets the need of the hungry.

THE MAN AND HIS MESSAGE

From <u>Triumphs of Faith</u> (Oakland, California), August 1925, pages 173-77. Preached at the Pentecostal Camp Meeting, Berkeley, California, and reported by O.C. Smith, Glad Tidings Temple, San Francisco.

"The best thing you ever could have is a great trial," Wigglesworth said. "It is your robing time. It is your coming into inheritance. Voice your position in God and you will be surrounded by all the resources of God in the time of trial. Shout, 'Get thee behind me, Satan,' and you will have the best time on earth. Whisper it and you won't."[1]

TWENTY-NINE

Lord, What Will You Have Me to Do?

Today I want to read from the ninth and nineteenth chapters of Acts, which record Paul's life-changing experience on the road to Damascus, his obedience to the Lord, and his God-given ministry. As soon as Paul saw the light from heaven outshining the brightness of the sun, he said, "Lord, what wilt thou have me to do?" (Acts 9:6). And as soon as he was willing to yield, he was in a condition where God could display his power, where God could have the man.

Oh, beloved, are you saying today, "What will you have me to do?" The place of yieldedness is just where God wants us. People are saying, "I want the baptism, I want healing, I would like to know of a certainty that I am a child of God." And I see nothing, absolutely nothing, in the way except unyieldedness to the plan of God. And that is what God wants from us today: obedience. When we begin yielding and yielding to God, he is able to fulfill his plan for our lives, and we come into that wonderful place where all we have to do is eat the fruits of Canaan.

After he had yielded to the lordship of Christ, Paul was given a mission to the whole of Asia. Later, as we read in the nine-teenth chapter, we know that Paul demanded certain conditions for the believers at Ephesus. He asked them, "Have ye received the Holy Ghost since ye believed?" (vs 2). When he laid hands on them, instantly they were filled with the Spirit and spoke in other tongues and prophesied (vs 6). The only thing needed was just to be in the condition where God could come in.

Brothers and sisters, it is the call of God that counts. Paul was in the call of God. Oh, I believe God wants to stir somebody's heart today to obedience. It may be for China, India, or Africa, but the thing God is looking for is obedience. "What will you have me to do?"

If God can have his way today, the ministry of somebody will begin; it always begins as soon as you yield. Paul had been bringing many people to prison, but God brought Paul to such a place of yieldedness and brokenness that he cried out, "What will you have me to do?" Paul's choice was to be a bond-servant for Jesus Christ.

Beloved, are you willing that God shall have his way today? Jesus said, "I will shew him how great things he must suffer for my name's sake" (Acts 9:16). But Paul saw that these things were working out a far more exceeding weight of glory. You people who have come for a touch from God, are you willing to follow him? Will you obey him?

When the prodigal son had returned and the father had killed the fatted calf and made a feast for him, the elder brother was angry and complained, "Thou never gavest me a kid, that I might make merry with my friends." But the father said to him, "All that I have is thine" (Luke 15:29-31). The elder brother could kill a fatted calf at any time. Beloved, all in the Father's house is ours, but it will come only through obedience. And when he can trust us, we will not come behind in anything.

Notice how God used Paul in Ephesus: "God wrought spe-cial miracles by the hand of Paul: So that from his body were brought unto the sick handkerchiefs or aprons, and the diseases departed from them, and the evil spirits went out of them" (vs 11-12). Let us notice the handkerchiefs that went forth from his body. When Paul touched and sent them forth, God wrought special miracles through them, and diseases departed from the sick, and evil spirits went out of the afflicted. Is it not lovely?

I believe that after we lay hands on these handkerchiefs and pray over them today, they should be handled very sacredly, and even as someone carries them, these handkerchiefs will bring life—if they are carried in faith to the suffering one. The very effect of it, if you only believe, would change your own body as you carry it.

A woman came to me one day and said, "My husband is such a trial to me. The first salary he gets he spends it in drink, and then he cannot do his work and comes home. I love him very much. What can be done?" I said, "If I were you I would take a handkerchief and would place it under his head when he goes to sleep at night, and say nothing to him, but have a living faith."

We anointed a handkerchief in the name of Jesus, and she put it under his head. Oh, beloved, there is a way to reach these wayward ones. The next morning on his way to work her husband stopped for a glass of beer. He lifted it to his lips but he thought there was something wrong with it; so he put it down and went out. He went to another saloon, and another, and did the same thing. At the end of the day he came home sober. His wife was gladly surprised to see him so, and he told her the story, how it had affected him. That was the turning point in this man's life. It meant not only giving up drink, but it also meant his salvation.

THE POWER OF SURRENDER

God wants to change our faith today. He wants us to see that it is not obtained by struggling and working and pining. Look at these promises from the Word: "The Father himself loves you"

(John 16:27). "Himself took our infirmities, and bare our sicknesses" (Matthew 8:17). "Come unto me all *ye* that labour and are heavy laden, and I will give you rest" (Matthew 11:28).

Who is the one that will take the place of Paul, and yield and yield and yield, until God so possesses him in such a way that from his body virtue shall flow to the sick and suffering? It will have to be the virtue of Christ that flows. Don't think there is some magic virtue in the handkerchief or you will miss the virtue. It is the living faith in the person who lays the handkerchief on the body, and the power of God through the faith.

Praise God we may lay hold of this living faith today. The blood has never lost its power. As we get in touch with Jesus, wonderful things will happen. And what else? We shall get nearer and nearer to him.

There is another side to it. "Exorcists took upon them to call over them which had evil spirits the name of the Lord Jesus, saying, 'We adjure you by Jesus whom Paul preacheth.' . . . And the evil spirit answered and said, 'Jesus I know, and Paul I know; but who are ye?'" (Acts 19:13-15).

I beseech you in the name of Jesus, especially those of you who are baptized, to awaken to the fact that you have power if God is with you. But there must be a resemblance between you and Jesus. The evil spirit said, "Jesus I know, and Paul I know, but who are you?"

Paul had the resemblance. You are not going to get it without having his presence; his presence changes you. You are not going to be able to get the results without the marks of the Lord Jesus. You must have the divine power within yourself; devils will take no notice of any power if they do not see the Christ. "Jesus I know, and Paul I know, but who are you?"

The difference between these men and Paul was that they had not the marks of Christ, so the manifestation of the power of Christ was not seen. Do you want power? Don't take the wrong way. Don't take it as power because you speak in tongues. And if God has given you revelations along certain lines, don't take that for the power. Or if you have even laid hands on the sick and they have been healed, don't take that for the power.

"The Spirit of the Lord God *is* upon me" (Luke 4:18a). That alone is the power. Don't be deceived. There is a place where you know the Spirit is upon you, so you will be able to do the works which are wrought by this blessed Spirit of God in you. And the manifestation of his power shall be seen, and people will believe in the Lord. What will make men and women believe the divine promises of God? Beloved, let me say to you today that God wants you to be ministering spirits, which means to be clothed with another power. And this divine power, you know when it is there, and you know when it goes forth.

The baptism of Jesus must bring us to have a single eye to the glory of God; everything else is wasted time and wasted energy. Beloved, we can reach it; it is a high mark, but we can get to it. You ask how? "What will you have me to do?" That is the plan. It means a perfect surrender to the call of God, and perfect obedience.

THE FRUIT OF SURRENDER

A young Russian came to England. He did not know the language but learned it quickly and was very much used and blessed of God. And as the wonderful manifestations of the power of God were seen, people pressed upon him to know the secret of his power. This man felt it was so sacred between him and God that he should not tell it, but they pressed him so much he finally said to them: "First God called me, and his presence was so precious, that I said to God at every call I would obey him. And I yielded, and yielded, and yielded, until I realized that I was simply clothed with another power altogether. And I realized that God took me—tongue, thoughts, and everything—so that it was not myself, but it was Christ working through me."

How many of you today have known that God has called you over and over and has put his hand upon you, but you have not yielded? How many of you have had the breathing of his power within you, calling you to prayer, and you have to confess you have failed?

I went to a house one afternoon where I had been called and met a man at the door. He said, "My wife has not been out of bed for eight months; she is paralyzed. She has been looking so much for you to come; she is hoping God will raise her up." I went in and rebuked the devil's power. She said, "I know I am healed; if you go out, I will get up."

I left the house, and went away not hearing anything more about her. I went to a meeting that night, and a man jumped up and said he had something he wanted to say. He had to leave to catch a train but wanted to talk first. "I come to this city once a week, and I visit the sick all over the city. There is a woman I have been visiting and I was very much distressed about her. She was paralyzed and has lain on that bed many months, but when I went there today she was up doing her work." I tell this story because I want you to see Jesus.

We had a letter which came to our house to say that a young man was very ill. Martin had been to our mission a few years before with a very bad foot; he had no shoe on, but a piece of leather fastened onto the foot. God healed him that day. Three years later, something else came upon this same man. What it was I don't know, but Martin's heart failed, and he was helpless. He could not rise or dress or do anything for himself, and in that condition he called his sister and told her to write and see if I would pray.

My wife said to go, that she believed God would give me that life. I went, and when I got to this place, I found the whole country expecting me. They had heard that when I came this man would be healed. When I arrived I met the man's sister, who was just home from the hospital. She said, "It is too late." "Is he alive?" I asked. "Yes, just alive."

I went in and put my hands upon him and said, "Martin." He just breathed slightly and whispered, "The doctor said if I move from this position I will never move again." "Do you know the Scripture says, 'God *is* the strength of my heart, and my portion forever?'" (Psalm 73:26). He said, "Shall I get up?"

I said no so that the day could be spent in prayer and ministering the Word. I found a great state of unbelief in that house but I saw Martin had faith to be healed. God held me there to pray for that place. I finally said to the family, "Get Martin's clothes ready; I believe he is to be raised up." I felt the unbelief. I went to the chapel and had prayer with a number of people, and before noon they too believed Martin would be healed.

When I returned to the house, I asked, "Are his clothes ready?" When they answered no, I said, "Oh, will you hinder God's working in this house?" I went into Martin's room alone. I told him, "I believe God will do a new thing today. I believe when I lay hands on you the glory of heaven will fill the place." I laid my hands on him in the name of the Father, Son, and Holy Ghost, and immediately the glory of the Lord filled the room. I went headlong to the floor and did not see what took place on the bed, or in the room, but this young man began to shout out, "Glory, glory!" And I heard him say, "For your glory, Lord."

Martin stood before me perfectly healed. He opened the door and said to his father, "Father, the Lord has raised me up." And the father fell to the floor and cried for salvation. His sister was also perfectly healed at that moment by the power of God in that house.

God wants us to see that the power of God coming upon people has something more in it than we have yet known. The power to heal and to baptize is in this place, but you must say, "Lord, what will you have me to do?" You say it is many months before the harvest. If you had the eyes of Jesus you would see that the harvest is already here.

The devil will say you can't have faith; you tell him he is a liar. The Holy Ghost wants to manifest Jesus through you. Oh, may you never be the same again! The Holy Spirit moving upon us will make us to be like him, and we will truly say, "Lord, what will you have me to do?"

THE MAN AND HIS MESSAGE

Originally titled "What Wilt Thou Have Me to Do?" from *Triumphs of Faith* (Oakland, California), October 1914, pages 227-30. Preached at the Montgomery's Monday meeting in Oakland on his first visit to America. Reported by Miss Sadie Cody.

When the twenty-year-old Wigglesworth was associated with the Salvation Army, he moved to Liverpool, where he felt a burden to help young people. Each week he would gather poor, barefoot, ragged, and hungry boys and girls in sheds along the docks. He was earning good money as a plumber, but he spent all of it to feed the children. "What meetings we had! Hundreds of them were saved," Wigglesworth said. He and a friend would also visit hospitals and the ships tied up at the docks. "God gave me a great heart for the poor.... I fasted all day every Sunday and prayed, and I never remember seeing less than fifty souls saved by the power of God in the meetings with the children, in the hospitals, on the ships, and in the Salvation Army."[1]

APPENDIX

Smith Wigglesworth Time-Line

Because no known Wigglesworth diaries are available, I have compiled this time-line from various books, advertisements, posters, magazine articles, and correspondence. Readers having additions or corrections may write to the editor in care of Servant Publications, P.O. Box 8617, Ann Arbor, MI 48107.

1859	Born in Menston, Yorkshire, England, June 10. Baptized in Anglican Church, December 4.[1]
1865	Worked in the fields at age six, pulling and cleaning turnips.
1866	At age seven began working in woolen mill twelve hours a day. No time for school.
1867	Converted in Menston Methodist Church where John Wesley had preached.
1872	Confirmed in Anglican Church, September 5, at age thirteen. Moved to Bradford.
1875	Associated with Salvation Army and Plymouth Brethren.
1876	Baptized by immersion at age seventeen.

1879	Worked with poor children in Liverpool through gospel services and feeding program. Supported himself as a plumber.
1882	Married Mary Jane "Polly" Featherstone. Their five children were Alice, Seth, Harold, Ernest, and George.
Early 1900s	He and Polly founded Bowland Street Mission, Bradford. Placed a flag outside proclaiming "Christ Died for Our Sins" on one side and "I Am the Lord that Healeth Thee" on the other.
1907	Baptized in the Holy Spirit October 28, 1907, at Sunderland through the laying on of hands. Began preaching but continued his plumbing business for income.
1912	Sunderland *Daily Echo,* May 31, reported Wigglesworth's healing meeting at All Saints Church.
1913	London *Daily Mirror,* May 16, published front-page story along with four photographs of seaside baptismal service conducted by Wigglesworth.
1913	Polly died. The bereaved husband asked God for a double portion of the Spirit.
1914	Traveled to the United States via Canada. Spoke at Stone Church in Chicago during June. Two months later preached for George and Carrie Judd Montgomery at Cazadero, located in redwood country about sixty miles north of San Francisco. Wigglesworth ordained by M.M. Pinson and Robert Craig, August 1. World War I began in Europe, which hampered travel.
1915	Back in England for Easter convention. Preached in London at first pentecostal Whitsuntide meeting. His son George died.

1920   Ministered in Europe for six months: France, Switzerland, Scandinavian countries. Jailed in Switzerland twice.

1921   Conducted meetings in Stockholm for Lewis Pethrus in April. Was arrested for laying hands on the sick. Charges dismissed with the order that he not lay hands on the sick in a mass meeting that Whitmonday.

1922   Traveled to Australia and New Zealand via Sri Lanka. Arrived in North Melbourne, Australia, February 16, 1922, with meeting that night. Preached in Wellington, New Zealand, in May. Wellington's *Dominion* published lengthy report under banner headlines, "Faith Healing. Extraordinary Scenes at Town Hall. The Deaf Made to Hear."[2] Newspaper *Sun* in Christchurch was very critical of meetings held at the invitation of Sydenham Gospel Mission. Went on to Dunedin (Settlers Hall and Princess Theater). Reported in Dunedin's *Evening Star,* June 15, 1922. Stayed in Dunedin until end of June. Returned to Wellington, where he began meetings in July. *Dominion* reporters checked out healing affidavits. Started San Diego, California, meetings October 2. "Dare to Believe God" was his theme for Union Pentecostal meeting in Chicago, October 29–November 12.

1923   Returned to New Zealand in October. Held meetings in Auckland, Palmerton North, Blenheim, and went on to Wellington on December 16. Attended Pentecostal Convention December 23-30.

1923   Returned to the United States for preaching tour, which included stops in Berkeley,

California, and Springfield, Missouri.

1924	Received ministerial credentials with the United States Assemblies of God at age sixty-five. Under his "special calling," he marked "evangelist-teacher." Gospel Publishing House published *Ever-Increasing Faith*.
1925	Traveled to South Africa during the year. Started meeting in Phoenix with H.L. Faulkner, Apostolic Temple, February 8; preached at Maria Woodworth-Etter Tabernacle, Indianapolis, February 14. Held meetings in England and Switzerland. Preached in Bethel Temple, Los Angeles.
1927	Returned to Australia and New Zealand. Was at Richmond Temple, Melbourne, during the spring. Testimonies of healings in 1922 meetings given.
1927	Conducted meetings in Aimee Semple McPherson's Angelus Temple in the fall and other churches in Southern California. Preached at Glad Tidings Temple, San Francisco, October 26-November 6; also at Carrie Judd Montgomery's Monday meeting, October 31.
1928	In the spring went to Switzerland, then returned to England for Whitsuntide convention. Put up a tent in London to minister with the Church of England.
1930	Ministered in the United States, including meetings with Robert and Marie Brown in New York. Sailed for home April 19.
1930-33	Suffered with gallstones. Refused to seek medical help.

1932	Asked the Lord for fifteen more years. Held meetings in Eureka Springs, Arkansas, August 29-September 12.
1933	Healed of gallstones, October 4.
1934	Returned to the United States in the fall.
1935	Wigglesworth—now 76 years old—and the Salters ministered at Glad Tidings Temple, San Francisco, January 29-February 10.
1936	Traveled to South Africa. Gave prophecy concerning David du Plessis.
1938	Gospel Publishing House published *Faith That Prevails*.
1939-47	Ministry confined to England because of World War II and his increasing age.
1943-48	Smith Wigglesworth died March 12, 1947, at Glad Tidings Hall, Wakefield, Yorkshire. Funeral held at Elim Church in Bradford, March 17. Would have been eighty-eight in June. Deaths of contemporary ministers included Stephen Jeffreys and A.J. Tomlinson, 1943; Aimee Semple McPherson, 1944; Carrie Judd Montgomery, 1946; Charles Price, 1947; E.W. Kenyon and Robert Brown, 1948.
1947-50	Other evangelists began salvation-healing ministries, including Kathryn Kuhlman, Oral Roberts, William Branham, Jack Coe, and A.A. Allen.

Notes

Foreword

1. Written for *Redemption Tidings* (Now *Redemption*) (Nottingham, England), as "Smith Wigglesworth," in a series, "Personal Memories of Our Pioneers," March 13, 1964, 5-6. Used by permission. Donald Gee (1891-1966) was an English preacher-teacher and wrote more than thirty books, including *Concerning Spiritual Gifts*.
2. Gee refers to the biography Frodsham wrote, *Smith Wigglesworth, Apostle of Faith*, published in 1948. *Ever-Increasing Faith* is the book of Wigglesworth's sermons which Frodsham compiled in 1924.
3. Contradictory accounts have been given of Wigglesworth's last words in the church vestry. Others say he inquired about the condition of a sick woman and then died.

Introduction

1. William Hacking, *Smith Wigglesworth Remembered* (Tulsa: Harrison, 1981), 20.
2. George Stormont, *Wigglesworth, A Man Who Walked with God* (Tulsa: Harrison, 1989), 65.
3. Colin C. Whittaker, "Smith Wigglesworth, The Apostle of Faith," chapter 1, *Seven Pentecostal Pioneers* (Springfield, Mo.: Gospel Publishing House, 1985), 17.
4. Hacking, 28-29.
5. Carl Brumback, *Suddenly... from Heaven* (Springfield, Mo.: Gospel Publishing House, 1961), 272.
6. Whittaker, 43.

7. *Looking Back to Our Future,* 1913-1988 (San Francisco, Calif.: Glad Tidings Temple, 1988), 43. Wigglesworth tells in his article "Wonderfully Healed" (*Triumphs of Faith,* January 1934, 10) of passing gallstones after a three-year struggle.

8. David du Plessis, *A Man Called Mr. Pentecost* (Plainfield, N.J.: Logos International, 1977), 2-3. Among his many contacts with people outside of the pentecostal movement, Du Plessis was received by three Roman Catholic pontiffs: John XXIII, Paul VI, and John Paul II. For more on Du Plessis and his ecumenical role, see Russell P. Spittler's article in the *Dictionary of Pentecostal and Charismatic Movements,* 250-54.

9. Stormont, 114.

PART One: Faith: A Gift for the Asking

ONE
What Is Faith?

1. Stanley Howard Frodsham, *Smith Wigglesworth, Apostle of Faith* (Springfield, Mo.: Gospel Publishing House, 1948), 111.

TWO
The Door to Life Eternal

1. In his eighty-sixth year, a year before he died, Wigglesworth believed God was again quickening him physically. He wrote to his old friend Stanley H. Frodsham, "My youth is being renewed like the eagle's, and so I am a man of action. I was preaching twice last Sunday just the same as I did years ago. You would be surprised at my youthful vigor. The Lord is making my ministry full of life and faith. I have no time to spend on anything earthly." Frodsham included the excerpt in *Pentecostal Evangel,* August 2, 1947, page 3, following Wigglesworth's death.

2. Stormont, 11.

THREE
Awake to Take!

1. W.H. Stuart-Fox, *Redemption Tidings* (London), July 1928, as quoted in Colin C. Whittaker, "Smith Wigglesworth," *Seven Pentecostal Pioneers* (Springfield, Mo.: Gospel Publishing House, 1985), 34-35. See also "The Man and His Message," Chapter 4, for another part of the vicar's report.

FOUR
Knowing God: The Key to Faith

1. Preaching this sermon in 1919, Wigglesworth refers to the influenza epidemic (1918-19), which killed about twenty million people, claiming more lives than did World War I.
2. Stuart-Fox, as quoted in Colin C. Whittaker, 35. See also "The Man and His Message," Chapter 3, for another part of the vicar's report.

FIVE
Building on the Word

1. Stanley H. Frodsham, *With Signs Following* (Springfield, Mo.: Gospel Publishing House, 1946), 223. John A.D. Adams, a supreme court attorney, was only one of many New Zealanders to be baptized in the Holy Spirit during these meetings. He authored two books, *The Voice of God Unheard* and *The Reason Why,* and another one on the baptism in the Holy Spirit. Reports on Wigglesworth's return to New Zealand and Australia in 1923 can be found in other publications, including *The Pentecostal Evangel,* January 5, 1924, in "Here and There," 7.

SIX
Keep Your Eyes Fixed on Jesus

1. Not used so much as in former times, "praying through" was understood as praying for a matter until the answer came—either by a visible sign, such as a healing, or an inward witness that God had heard and had given peace about the matter.

SEVEN
A Living Hope

1. Whittaker, 29-31. Pastor Pethrus later built the thirty-five-hundred-seat Filadelphia Church and invited Wigglesworth back for other campaigns.

Part Two: Putting Faith into Action

NINE
Making a Pest of Yourself

1. *Looking Back to Our Future,* 42.

TEN
Faith That Delivers

1. *Looking Back to Our Future*, 42.

ELEVEN
Become an Overcomer

1. Stormont, 77.

TWELVE
Children of Circumstances or Children of Faith?

1. "A Close-Up of Smith Wigglesworth," an undated clipping from *The Religious Press*, written by an "M.S.," in Wigglesworth collection, Assemblies of God Archives.

THIRTEEN
Pressing through to Victory

1. David W. Dories, "The Making of Smith Wigglesworth," Part 2, *Assemblies of God Heritage*, Winter 1992-93, 22.

FOURTEEN
Doing the Works of Jesus

1. Philip B. Duncan, *The Charismatic Tide*, as quoted by Dennis and Gwen Smith in *A River Is Flowing* (St. Agnes, South Australia: Assemblies of God in Australia, 1987), 21-22.

FIFTEEN
Be Not Afraid, Only Believe

1. James Salter, "He Was Not... God Took Him," *Redemption Tidings* (London), March 28, 1947, 1. Reprinted in *The Evangelist* (Baton Rouge, La.), March 1988, 21, 22.

Part Three: Receiving Power from on High

SIXTEEN
The Resurrection Touch

1. "Our Union Meetings," *Latter Rain Evangel* (Stone Church, Chicago), December 1922, 12. It was said that the union meetings were the first among pentecostal congregations in Chicago and were held in a three-thousand-seat church building owned by the Volunteers of America. Wigglesworth's slogan for the meetings was "Dare to Believe God." The November 1922 issue of the magazine stated Wigglesworth's focus: "He has a three-fold message—salvation, healing, and the baptism of the Holy Ghost—and he emphasizes all in each meeting."

SEVENTEEN
Filled with New Wine

1. The wine in Palestine was kept in wineskins, which in time lost their elasticity, and so would split when the new wine fermented. New wine must be in new wineskins.
2. Hacking, 30.

EIGHTEEN
The Place of Power

1. Lewi Pethrus, *Personal Memoirs* (Stockholm), vol. 3, 542, as quoted in Whittaker, 29.

NINETEEN
The Ordinary Made Extraordinary

1. Wigglesworth suffered intense pain for three years due to gallstones until they finally passed. Even so, it appears that his views on healing remained the same, except that a request for healing could be delayed—as was true in his case.
2. Michael Harper, *As at the Beginning* (Plainfield, N.J.: Logos International, 1971), 46.

TWENTY
Showing Forth the Glory of God

1. Stanley H. Frodsham, editor's note, "Ye Shall Receive Power," *Pentecostal Evangel*, August 2, 1947, 3.

TWENTY-ONE
God's Treasure House

1. David W. Dories notes that Wigglesworth parted company with some classical pentecostals, and this is one example. See "The Making of Smith Wigglesworth," Part 2, *Assemblies of God Heritage,* Winter 1992-93, 21.
2. Harper, 42. Wigglesworth never forgot Polly's contribution to his spiritual and educational development. He would often say, "All that I am today, I owe under God, to my precious wife."

TWENTY-TWO
Aflame for God

1. Stanley H. Frodsham, *With Signs Following,* 101-2.

Part Four: Yielding to the Holy Spirit

TWENTY-FOUR
Living Epistles of Christ

1. Several authors have perpetuated the error that Wigglesworth never belonged to a denomination, but he belonged to at least one. Records at the American Assemblies of God show him as ordained (1924-29), and that he was ordained during his visit to California in 1914. For some reason he did not renew his annual membership when it came due in 1929, and he was listed as lapsed. When he wrote to renew in 1930, the policy had changed so that if one's country had its own pentecostal organization which was amicable with the American Assemblies of God—which Great Britain had—membership in the American group was no longer permitted. This did not, however, affect his relationship with the American denomination; they continued inviting him to their churches and published his sermons and news in their *Pentecostal Evangel.*

TWENTY-SIX
Rising into the Heavenlies

1. Stormont, 33.

TWENTY-SEVEN
The Privileges of Sonship

1. Stanley Howard Frodsham, *Smith Wigglesworth, Apostle of Faith* (Springfield, Mo.: Gospel Publishing House, 1948), 68-69. Salter was married to Wigglesworth's daughter Alice and was a missionary to the Congo (now Zaire).

TWENTY-EIGHT
Count It All Joy

1.   Whittaker, 22.

TWENTY-NINE
Lord, What Will You Have Me To Do?

1.   Frodsham, *Smith Wigglesworth, Apostle of Faith,* 15-16.

Appendix
Smith Wigglesworth Time-Line

1.   James Salter gave June 8, 1859, as Wigglesworth's birthday.
2.   *Dominion,* May 31, 1922. Perplexing to the Wigglesworth family is that while many people reportedly were healed in the meetings, Alice Wigglesworth Salter—who traveled with her father at times—remained deaf throughout her life.

BIBLIOGRAPHY

Additional Reading on
Smith Wigglesworth

Forty years after Smith Wigglesworth's death, no fewer than eight books about him, or containing his sermons, were available. *Cry of the Spirit* and this book have brought the total to ten. Perhaps others will follow. With the exception of Roberts Liardon, these English authors or compilers knew Wigglesworth personally and had heard him preach. To help you better understand the man they called the "Apostle of Faith," I have used incidents from these and other sources for "The Man and His Message" at the end of each sermon in this book.

Frodsham, Stanley Howard. *Smith Wigglesworth, Apostle of Faith*. Springfield, Mo.: Gospel Publishing House, 1948. Also published by the Assemblies of God of Great Britain and Ireland in 1949. Written by his old friend and published the year after Wigglesworth's death, this biography contains his own story as told to Frodsham during a meeting in Riverside, California.

Hacking, William. *Smith Wigglesworth Remembered*. Tulsa: Harrison, 1981. Published in 1972 as *Reminiscences of*

Smith Wigglesworth. Hacking focuses on his old friend's "Great Challenge to Daring Faith."

Hibbert, Albert. *Smith Wigglesworth: The Secret of His Power.* Tulsa: Harrison, 1982. A friend's attempt at analyzing Wigglesworth's spiritual power.

Hywel-Davies, Jack. *The Life of Smith Wigglesworth.* Ann Arbor, Mich.: Servant, 1987. A well-researched biography by an English minister and writer. This book was originally published by Hodder and Stoughton, London, as *Baptised by Fire* in 1987.

Liardon, Roberts. *Cry of the Spirit.* Laguna Hills, Calif.: Roberts Liardon Ministry, 1991. Originally published by Harrison, Tulsa, 1990.

Stormont, George. *Wigglesworth, A Man Who Walked with God.* Tulsa: Harrison, 1989. A brief biography by a minister who knew Wigglesworth and would often lecture about him.

Whittaker, Colin C. *Seven Pentecostal Pioneers.* Springfield, Mo.: Gospel Publishing House, 1985. Editor of *Redemption* (formerly *Redemption Tidings*), Nottingham, England, Whittaker has included a chapter on Wigglesworth: "Smith Wigglesworth, The Apostle of Faith." Originally published in 1983 by Edward England Books.

Wigglesworth, Smith. *Ever-Increasing Faith.* Springfield, Mo.: Gospel Publishing House, 1924, 1971. Contains eighteen sermons which Wigglesworth preached in Springfield, Missouri, and which had been taken down in shorthand.

Wigglesworth, Smith. *Faith That Prevails.* Springfield, Mo.: Gospel Publishing House, 1938. Seven more sermons taken in shorthand and published in book form.